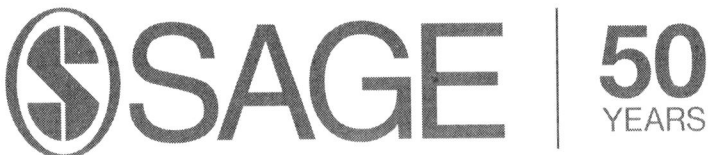

SAGE was founded in 1965 by Sara Miller McCune to support the dissemination of usable knowledge by publishing innovative and high-quality research and teaching content. Today, we publish more than 750 journals, including those of more than 300 learned societies, more than 800 new books per year, and a growing range of library products including archives, data, case studies, reports, conference highlights, and video. SAGE remains majority-owned by our founder, and on her passing will become owned by a charitable trust that secures our continued independence.

Los Angeles | London | Washington DC | New Delhi | Singapore

My Half of the Sky

My Half of the Sky

12 Life Stories of Courage

Indrani Raimedhi

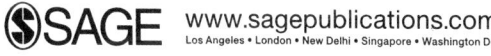

www.sagepublications.com
Los Angeles • London • New Delhi • Singapore • Washington DC

First published in 2015 by

 SAGE Publications India Pvt Ltd
B1/I-1 Mohan Cooperative Industrial Area
Mathura Road, New Delhi 110 044, India
www.sagepub.in

SAGE Publications Inc
2455 Teller Road
Thousand Oaks, California 91320, USA

SAGE Publications Ltd
1 Oliver's Yard, 55 City Road
London EC1Y 1SP, United Kingdom

SAGE Publications Asia-Pacific Pte Ltd
3 Church Street
#10-04 Samsung Hub
Singapore 049483

Published by Vivek Mehra for SAGE Publications India Pvt Ltd, typeset in 11/14 Bembo by RECTO Graphics, Delhi, and printed at Saurabh Printers Pvt Ltd, New Delhi.

Library of Congress Cataloging-in-Publication Data Available

ISBN: 978-93-515-0037-7 (HB)

The SAGE Team: Rudra Narayan, Neha Sharma, Rajib Chatterjee, and Rajinder Kaur

To the truly enlightened man
who is proud of a woman's strength

Thank you for choosing a SAGE product! If you have any comment, observation or feedback, I would like to personally hear from you. Please write to me at <u>contactceo@sagepub.in</u>

—Vivek Mehra, Managing Director and CEO,
SAGE Publications India Pvt Ltd, New Delhi

Bulk Sales

SAGE India offers special discounts for purchase of books in bulk. We also make available special imprints and excerpts from our books on demand.

For orders and enquiries, write to us at

Marketing Department
SAGE Publications India Pvt Ltd
B1/I-1, Mohan Cooperative Industrial Area
Mathura Road, Post Bag 7
New Delhi 110044, India
E-mail us at <u>marketing@sagepub.in</u>

Get to know more about SAGE, be invited to SAGE events, get on our mailing list. Write today to <u>marketing@sagepub.in</u>

This book is also available as an e-book.

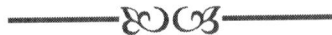

Contents

Foreword

The Northeast was for many in the "heartland" a faraway and somewhat mysterious place at the time of Independence. Less so with the passage of time. Even so, Indrani Raimedhi has rendered a signal service by revealing another facet of this very diverse region through a series of fascinating stories of some of its remarkable women, exemplars all.

Although seen at the forefront in many parts of the Northeast, the notion that, unlike their sisters in most other parts of the country, northeastern women necessarily enjoy a greater degree of freedom and an equal and even privileged position in society is exaggerated. This is so even in Meghalaya's matrilineal society where the youngest uncle controls the purse. *My Half of the Sky* narrates stories of indomitable women who have fought privation, discrimination, and adversities of every kind to become icons and blaze new trails.

Jahnabi was tricked into marrying an AIDS victim from a privileged Assamese home, only to be ostracized and widowed and herself infected as a young mother. Though shunned by society, she fought for her rights, joined Indian Network of Positive People, and found Assam Network of Positive People in 2002. Her message to every women: "don't match horoscopes before marriage but go for a blood test." Urmee Mazumdar likewise bravely fought polio and found Swabalambi (self-reliant) in rural Assam to train people with all manners of disability to stand on their own feet. Bertha Dkhar of Shillong, a blind person herself, developed a Khasi Braille and launched a campaign for inclusive education for all in normal schools.

The differently abled do not want sympathy but facilities for training so that they can lead normal lives and cultivate their talents. These three women have shown the way.

Others like Birubala Rabha have fought witch-hunting, a terrible scourge in rural India, where quack "medicine-men" are quick to label any innocent woman as a witch and beat and torment her to death to exculpate their own superstitions and criminal folly. Mary Kom became an Olympic boxer, winning laurels for Manipur and India. And, Parbati, a zamindar's daughter, became India's first and best-known woman elephant mahout. Hasina Kharbhih has fought child and female trafficking, a heart-rending but flourishing criminal trade across porous international and state borders.

And then there are writers, journalists, filmmakers, and human rights defenders like Monalisa Changkija and Manju Baruah who probe and mirror the Northeastern reality. Novelist Rita Chowdhury documented the Assam anti-foreigner movement, and has written movingly about the indignity and wrong done by the Indian state to the small, hard-working, and well-integrated Chinese community, long domiciled around Makum in north Assam, by exiling them to western India in 1962 on security considerations. Teresa Rehman has reported courageously and objectively from the Northeast and now runs an online journal Thumbprintmag.com to tell the world about what goes on there. Her story, telling of a daylight fake encounter in Manipur brought her both kudos and threats. Monisha Behal founded the very useful Northeast Network that has empowered women.

Indrani's pen portraits of these pioneering women achievers make them and their work come alive. She writes with a human touch—about how ordinary women have achieved greatness and of the greatness inherent in ordinary women.

My Half of the Sky is a valuable addition to literature on the Northeast. Indeed, it portrays the story of all Indian women and the relentless struggle the country must wage to invest people with dignity.

B.G. Verghese
Senior fellow, Centre for Policy Research

Introduction

Journalism is about the here and the now, and fiction is about the universal and the timeless. If writing is a solitary occupation, then journalism is just the opposite—you interact with people all the time. I had spent 25 tough, memorable years trying to be both a writer and a journalist before the idea of writing this book became a gleam in my eye. An idea travels through the invisible routes of the subconscious before it emerges, fully formed. Writing this book is an intrinsic part of not only who I am, but more importantly, where I come from.

I am an Assamese, belonging to Assam, one of the states of what is known as India's Northeast region. It is a part of the country idealized in glossy tourist brochures, overlooked by the powers-that-be, and utterly unknown to the average Indian. It is a region that is far away in every sense of the term—whether it be in physical distance, accessibility, or cultural affinity. The eight states are clubbed together under a common name that does not take into account the individual identities, cultures, and ethnicities of each state. As if it was not troubling enough to be in the periphery, Northeast India began to feature in mainstream Indian media for all the wrong reasons—insurgency, bomb blasts, ethnic violence, kidnapping, secret killings, and reprisal of armed forces. The picture of emerald hills, sparkling waterfalls, and virgin forests was stained with blood. There were heartbreaking stories of families separated, homes destroyed, and brother turning against brother. Like other writers in this troubled region, I too wrote stories depicting the horrors of this grim reality.

I struggled to convey what it was to be a woman at this point of history in this corner of the world. And then gradually, I realized that it was real stories of real women that were waiting to be narrated, stories that go beyond clichés and hype to reveal the indomitable spirit of woman. The 12 women featured in this book challenge traditional views about women's place in society and the home. They prove that Indian women are boldly stepping out of their marginalized space. They have confronted great odds and endured heartbreaking ordeals to stand by what they believe in. Their stirring narratives dispel gender stereotypes and reveal facets of this beautiful, troubled part of the country. This book also stands for the premise that all issues are women issues.

One of my favorite authors, Virginia Woolf, commented with great perspicacity that "For much of history, Anonymous was a woman." It indeed is still true of women who hail from this corner of the nation. And yet, Gandhiji himself had praised Assamese women for weaving fairy tales on their looms. We have had heroic women like Ahom warrior Mula Gabharu, Ahom Queen Phuleswari, and martyrs like Kanaklata who lived and died for freedom. Many a time, such women are relegated to footnotes in dusty tomes. Our knowledge of their lives is restricted to some flimsy anecdotes, a few stereotyped images, some exotic notions, and most often, a recalling of grim facts. How does a woman of today's Northeast perceive the reality of a lived experience? How are they meeting the challenges of finding their voice and making their lives meaningful? How are they discarding the tag of victimhood to make miracles possible? It was to find out answers to these questions that I plunged into the writing of this book.

The challenges were evident much before I put pen to paper. Who were the women that I would shortlist to feature in my book? The women studies cell of a prestigious local college had already produced a book titled, *Assamese Woman—The Pathbreakers*. It had brief biographical sketches of women social workers, writers, academicians, dancers, artists, entrepreneurs, doctors, and so on, all neatly pigeon-holed. But the book I had in mind was to be about drama in real life, about women who would lay bare intimate details of their lives, and take me along the journeys they had made from the known to the unknown.

Having grown up in an undivided Assam, I had mingled joyously with Khasi, Naga, Manipuri, Lushai, and Karbi children. In my lifetime I have seen separate states carved out of Assam like pieces of a jigsaw puzzle, the pieces must fit for a jigsaw puzzle to make sense. And one way to do it was to reach out to Bertha Dkhar from Meghalaya, Monalisa Changkija from Nagaland, and Mary Kom from Manipur. Logistical constraints did not permit me to find role models to represent Tripura, Arunachal Pradesh, Mizoram, and Sikkim. Assam has been represented by Parbati Barua, Teresa Rehman, Jahnabi Goswami, Monisha Behal, and Birubala Rabha. This apparent overrepresentation of my home state Assam has more to do with opportunities of access to them than a natural bias. Anshu Jensempa, the first woman from the Northeast to scale Mt. Everest twice seemed always as distant as the lonely snow-clad peaks. A brief telephone conversation with her and some YouTube clips could not be stretched to a fitting narrative. A distinguished legal luminary's work in her field is enriching beyond measure, but would readers pore over reams of legal terms and references, without a gripping back story? After several interviews and much note-taking, that chapter was shelved, and so was the chapter about an admired and internationally recognized disarmament activist. If there was one thing I was determined to avoid, it was cobbling together a string of hagiographies.

As I waded out to the uncharted sea, the perils became quickly apparent. Almost all the women were known to me, and as much as they agreed to be interviewed, they could not give me time. Jahnabi Goswami was setting up a home for HIV positive orphans. Bertha Dkhar was not keen on my visiting her in Shillong on a Sunday because she was a regular churchgoer. Parbati Barua often vanished without a trace to the heart of jungles far from the city to be with her beloved elephants, leaving me in the lurch. A giant billboard in front of my office showed Mary Kom at her pugnacious best, and I had to use my imagination, videos, and newspaper reports to script her enthralling story. From faraway Dimapur, a town in Nagaland, Monalisa Changkija patiently answered my questions on an e-mail, and these were used to create an imaginary encounter between her and Tanya Chopra, a Delhi-based journalist. Being a writer of the fiction genre, I made use of such devices in my attempt to give the account a compelling immediacy and context. The sheer breadth and depth of writer activist Rita Chowdhury's work made great demands on me as I struggled to record her life and her beliefs. A great lot of material already existed on her, but in this account her honesty and erudition shines through. Teresa has been a close friend and active editorial collaborator in this book. Shy of talking about her achievements, it took a lot of gentle coaxing and implacable ultimatums for her to go through her life and work. Teresa's story is all the more remarkable, hailing us she does from a minority community that still imposes many strictures on women.

There is a definite element of serendipity in my being able to get in touch with anti-witchcraft crusader Birubala Rabha. But when we spoke on the phone, she could not understand what it was I wanted from her. Finally, I made myself understood. She was to come and see me in Guwahati, be a guest at my home, and tell her story for a book. One rainy afternoon, she arrived at my door. Hours of conversation became possible through an interpreter, and I finally had my story. Urmee Mazumdar and I had long nightly phone conversations. We lived 10 minutes away from each other. Somewhere along the way, I stopped having a plan and went with the flow, interviewing whoever was free at the moment. So there I was, writing multiple narratives, simultaneously, sometimes finding myself stonewalled and at other times feeling it was as effortless as a walk in the park. As months passed, the manuscript grew, and we became this broad informal group of 13 women, making ourselves heard, sharing our experiences, and completing the jigsaw puzzle.

All through the writing of this book, I remembered the words of Bohemian American activist and writer Anais Nin, who, with searing honesty, challenged, "How wrong is it for a woman to expect the man to build the world she wants, rather than to create it herself?" These 12 women had built, often from snatch, edifices that are a triumph of the human spirit.

In order to appreciate better the struggles of these 12 women, it is necessary to remember that like millions of others in this troubled corner of the country, these women too suffered the privations of a long, unending conflict. Northeast India has been the theater of the earliest and most prolonged insurgency in the country. Independent demands started in Naga Hills, then still a part of Assam, as far back as in 1952. This was shortly followed by the Mizo rebellion in 1966. The late 1970s saw the emergence of more separatist outfits, including the United Liberation Front of Assam (UFLA) and the National Democratic Force of Bodoland. Except for Sikkim, all the other seven states of the region are affected by insurgent violence. Author and political commentator Wasbir Hussain, in his book *Home-makers without the Men*, describes how in any conflict situation women and children are drawn into the vortex of the problem. He cites numerous instances of husbands, sons, and brothers, besides the women themselves, getting killed either at the hands of militants or the security forces who battle these militants. In some cases, terrorists have slain civilians in this deadly cocktail of hate and suspicion. Hundreds of insurgent cadres have been neutralized by the security forces during anti–insurgency operations. Security personnel have also lost their lives. One is haunted by the fact there are countless families across the Northeast who have lost their breadwinner—be it a father, a brother, or a husband. Women of these families have had to put aside their grief to make a living, raise their children, and rebuild their shattered homes. Organizations such as Mothers Union in Meghalaya, the

Naga Mothers Association, the Naga Women's Union, and Meira Paibis in Manipur have struggled long and hard to restore sanity in a fractured land. Peace processes have been initiated by government and civil society groups, with mixed results. Jnanpith award winner Dr Mamoni Raisom Goswami, with her apolitical credentials and integrity, acted as the mediator between the Union government and the ULFA at a crucial period in Assam's recent history.

The icon of public resistance who has been the most visible symbol of our collective predicament is Irom Sharmila Chanu, a civil right activist and poet from Manipur. On November 11, 2000 she began a hunger strike which continues till date. Described as the world's longest hunger striker, this implacable warrior of peace is on trial for attempted suicide. Her protest can be traced to a horrifying incident on November 11, 2000, when 10 civilians were shot down in cold blood as they were standing at a bus stop. This Malom Massacre was allegedly carried out by the Assam Rifles, one of the divisions of the Indian military forces operating in the state. One of the victims, ironically, was the 18-year-old Sinam Chandramani Singh, a 1986 Child Bravery Award winner. Lacerated by the incident, Irom Sharmila began her fast from that very day. Three days later, she was arrested by the police with an attempt to commit suicide, which is unlawful under the Indian Penal Code. She has been regularly released and rearrested every year since her hunger strike began. This frail and valiant woman has waged a nonviolent struggle to ensure the repeal of the Armed Forces Special Power Act (AFSPA). On July 15, 2004, some women activists of the Meira Paibis stripped in front of the Kangla Fort, the headquarter of the Assam Rifles in Manipur, triggering an unprecedented civil disobedience in Manipur against the AFSPA, 1958, which led to the establishment of a review committee to examine this act. The protests were against the alleged extrajudicial execution of Thangjam Manorama Devi on the night of

July 11, 2004, by the Assam Rifles and to repeal the AFSPA. The AFSPA empowers the representative of the central government, the governor, to subsume the powers of the state government to declare undefined disturbed areas. It also empowers the noncommissioned officers of the armed forces to arrest without warrant, to destroy any structure that may be hiding absconders, without any verification, to conduct search and seizure without warrant, and to even shoot to death. What is more troubling, no legal proceeding against abuse of such arbitrary powers can be initiated without the prior permission of the central government. While introducing the AFSPA on August 18, 1958, the government accepted it as an emergency measure, and it was supposed to have been in force only for a year.

Where does my group of women figure in all this? Like others, they have been under the shadow of the eclipse. They have struggled to hold onto the quotidian assurances of a normal life. They have negotiated their way between uncertainties to bring meaning to their lives and the lives of others. Seen in this wider context, their trajectories assume a new meaning and resonance. Writing about them has been my way of rejoicing in what is good and courageous and noble in the midst of so much tragedy. And I, in all humility second American artist Georgia O'Keefe that "I feel there is something unexplored about women that only a woman can explore."

The 12 women who feature in this book come from diverse backgrounds. The thread that binds their stories is their resolve to change the circumstances of their lives, overcoming tremendous odds, and give wings to their dreams. They are survivors and pathfinders, doers, and dreamers, leaving in their wake surging inspiration and hope. Their testimonies reveal what it is like to live in this often forgotten corner of India. They have overcome personal tragedy, broken the falters of tradition, fought discrimination, and coped bravely with the harrowing experience of violence and uncertainty. Through the prism of these true life stories, I have also tried to explore the paradoxes, problems, triumphs, and realities of today's Indian woman.

Jahnabi Goswami is a radiant bride who steps into her husband's home, unaware of the terrible secret he is hiding from her. In a couple of years she loses him and her baby daughter to AIDS. She then takes the unprecedented step of coming out into the open as the first HIV positive woman from the Northeast and sets up the Assam Network of Positive People. Jahnabi reveals how she refused to don the tag of victim and struggles against great odds to help people with HIV/AIDS and fight for their rights. She has transformed herself from a shattered widow and a grieving mother to a powerhouse of energy—counseling patients, coordinating with different agencies, and traveling all over the world, being a passionate spokesperson for people with HIV/AIDS. She embodies feminine strength and resilience in the face of dark adversity.

Parbati Barua is the celebrated Elephant Queen, the only woman elephant trainer in the world. Born into an affluent and privileged zamindar family, she chose to answer the call of the wild, taming elephants, and training them. Her daredevil exploits deep in the inaccessible jungles have captured the imagination of the world. In this exclusive and free-wheeling interview, the reclusive and enigmatic Parbati offers a compelling view of her extraordinary life and her mystical bond with these majestic creatures.

As a teenager Rita Chowdhury spent years as a fugitive student revolutionary hiding from the law. She went on to chronicle the Assam movement against foreign nationals, capturing in gripping prose the drama of those stirring years. Her novel *Deo Langkhui*, an epic work and a historical fiction on the Tiwa tribe of Assam, won her the Sahitya Akademi Award. With her writing committed to the cause of the voiceless, Chowdhury brings to light a dark chapter of the Indo-China war of 1962, when the Chinese Indians of Upper Assam were forcibly transported to an internment camp in Rajasthan. She uses her remarkable storytelling powers to point out the injustice done to these forgotten people.

Award-winning journalist Teresa Rehman risks her life to uncover explosive stories in India's troubled Northeast. Penetrating deep into a jungle camp to interview an elusive dreaded rebel leader or exposing to world a shocking encounter killing in broad daylight by the state forces, it is all part of Teresa's usual work schedule. Teresa continues to be driven by her commitment to report on issues unknown to the rest of the country and the world. With her ear to the ground, Teresa works to reveal the many facets of the region and feels strongly that every story must be in the larger interest of the society.

Afflicted by polio when she was a toddler, Urmee Mazumdar has always refused to make compromises or seek the easy way out. Her life has been dedicated to working among the disabled through her NGO, Swabalambi, making them aware of their rights, arranging for their treatment, and training them for a livelihood. Because of her efforts, hundreds of differently abled people have learnt to lead meaningful lives. And Urmee continues to win awards for her valiant crusade.

How does one feel when one's world turns dark, familiar faces vanish, and every step ahead seems an abyss? Ask Bertha G. Dkhar, the Khasi lady who turned blind just when life was beckoning her with its many promises. Bertha traveled from fear, heartbreak, rage, and, eventually, to acceptance. Along the way, her heart went out to others like her—blind boys and girls. Against great odds, she created Braille in the Khasi language and ushered in a quiet revolution in the area of education for the visually challenged. Honored with the Padmashree, Bertha Dkhar is today a pillar of the Khasi society and an inspiring role model.

Mary Kom, the daughter of an impoverished farmer's family in a Manipur village, does something unprecedented that puts her on the long road to international fame as an Olympic boxer. Her grit and tenacity leads her from one victory to another even as the dice seems loaded against her. Find out the Biblical story that has been the bedrock of Mary's unshakeable faith in herself.

On a still moonlit night, a lone woman sets out on a journey to save a life. Birubala Rabha is the feisty crusader who calls spade a spade and has tirelessly spoken out against witchcraft in Assam's remote countryside. This illiterate and poor woman has battled great odds to save 35 people, deemed witches and punished to death by superstitious villagers, from certain death. And she has willingly paid the price for her stance; she has not only been ostracized but even had to face death threats. Her courage and conviction continue to inspire many.

Concerned by rising instances of human trafficking, Meghalaya's Hasina Kharbhih has created the Meghalaya Model, a collective initiative involving government, NGOs, judiciary, police, and so on, which work in close collaboration to tackle the menace. Her work threatens the interests of traffickers, and they make death threats on the telephone, stalk her, and even try to push her in front of a moving vehicle. But Hasina is not one to back out, and today she is internationally recognized for her work.

A feisty Naga, Monalisa Changkija, upholds the values of free, fair, and fearless journalism as she struggles to bring out her daily newspaper against all odds.

Manju Borah makes waves as an award-winning director of films that are redolent of the spirit of the Northeast. Her work brings fresh hope to the crippled Assamese film industry. Unfazed by lack of finance and limited infrastructure, Manju continues to make films that touch on sensitive issues, resonating in viewers, cutting across cultures.

To Dr Monisha Behal goes the credit of single-handedly professionalizing social work in the Northeast. Northeast Network, her brainchild, is the leading NGO working in the area of women's rights. The chapter discussing Dr Behal traces the roots of her activism to her childhood.

Meeting these 12 remarkable women, being privy to their stories of struggle, hope, despair, and triumph, has been an experience of a lifetime. They together embody the face of the Northeast women—traditional, yet modern, tremendously resilient, and capable of enduring all odds. Yet it is necessary to also acknowledge that they go beyond the confines of a geographical place. Their stories are bound to inspire anyone, from any part of the world. As Virginia Woolf put it so eloquently, "As a woman I have no country. As a woman, I want no country. As a woman, my country is the whole world."

1

Betrayed by Love: Jahnabi Goswami

In the dying light of a long July evening, my friend Nandita and I are walking along one of the most beautiful roads of the city, toward the hills and lush wilderness of Krishnanagar, Guwahati. Flanked by sedate houses with pretty front gardens lined with lovingly tended earthen pots, leafy shrubs, and handkerchief lawns, the area has an old-world feel, as if it was a place time forgot. Children careen down the gentle slope in bicycles and neighbors are chatting amiably, leaning on their gates, fanning themselves, appearing in no hurry to end the day.

Walking up an incline, we find ourselves there. Circling a concrete yard, there are several box like building blocks, squat, and very utilitarian. We mount two flights of steps of the Krishnanagar Housing Complex and I press the bell of flat no. 4. Immediately, the sound of footsteps, a quick drawing back of the bolt, and Jahnabi Goswami opens the door, smiling her warm, cheery welcome. It is a Sunday evening, but this hyperactive young woman is fretting that she cannot be at several places at once. House-bound thanks to her car that broke down a week ago, Jahnabi has no option but to sit still and retrace the strange winding path of her life, a life that has been taken away from her, a life lived in the shadow of an eclipse. She has known betrayal, cruelty, abandonment. But in her story, the stuff of fiction, there is also great stoicism and grace under fire. She has picked up the pieces of her life and thrown away the tag of being the victim. So much so that today Jahnabi is an icon not only among AIDS survivors but all womanhood, for her actions embody the tenacity and resilience of those of her kind.

Jahnabi Goswami could have been a statistic. She may well have been the tragic figure of a morality tale. The scales of destiny were cruelly weighed against her. Cornered and humiliated for being HIV positive, Jahnabi fought back and scripted her remarkable story, the story of one who is the poster girl of AIDS survival and awareness. When Jahnabi became the first woman from Northeast India to openly declare herself as a HIV positive, she did it with the awareness that the world would recoil from her, ostracize her, refuse to let her be. But, with her beloved father killed by insurgents, a husband and daughter dead of AIDS, and her husband's family throwing her out of the house, what else was there to lose?

Appearances can be deceptive. Jahnabi's cozy flat has a comfortable sofa set and a divan with an ornate brocade cover. There is a laminated photograph of a remarkably handsome man, her father, on a side table. The fridge hums on the other side of a curtained screen. Jahnabi wears an aubergine-color top, teamed up with a floral sarong. She is fresh after a bath, her curly shoulder length hair still damp. She serves us tea and delicious jackfruit cookies, guffawing at how she hit upon the recipe when her mixie got cranky. She could pass off as yet another smart singleton living on her own in the city. But Jahnabi is a widow. She is a mother who lost her two-year-old Kasturi to AIDS. She was turned out of 11 rented houses by hostile landlords before Assam Chief Minister Tarun Gogoi allotted this flat to her. Plump and effervescent, she looks the picture of good health. She is on regular anti-retroviral therapy to keep the HIV under control.

American poet Wally Robert Doty, HIV positive, wrote about the word AIDS in his poem *Atlantis*.

"Not even a real word/But an acronym, a vacant, four letter cipher/That draws meaning into itself/reconstitutes the world."

As in this corner of the world little Jahnabi played in the green fields of her native Kampur, the shadow of AIDS loomed suddenly and frighteningly across the world. It is against this backdrop that Jahnabi's narrative must be understood.

Sipping a cup of tea, she begins.

"I was born at Kampur, and I have two younger sisters and a brother. We were a huge family of uncles, aunts, cousins living together in an ancestral house that had 11 bedrooms. There was always something to do, someone to talk to. In those early years, I did not know what loneliness meant. As a child I was full of mischief. Even today my family talks about how, when I was only two, would try cleansing our family *puja* room with water, basil leaves, imitating my grandfather, even reciting some Sanskrit *shloka*s. I would feel very important doing it." She laughs and puts down her tea cup. The dusk falls gently outside. Jahnabi's eyes are luminous with the light of other days. "Those were the happiest days of my life. I loved to eat and found it great fun to raid the neighbors' kitchens, escaping with things like coconut *laroo*s and milk powder from Amulspray tins. But of course I had to be taught a lesson, and it happened when I swallowed a whole lot of a white powder—washing soda, which I mistook for Amulspray!"

Jahnabi's family owned 22 *bigha*s (measurement of land) in the village. Farmers tilled their fields, and there were orchids of fruit trees, betel nut trees, and ponds alive with fish. Uncle Nripen Goswami was a senior congress leader and a former member of parliament. All through her girlhood years, she was used to people visiting their home at all hours of the day to confer on matters of state. There were also many family excursions to Dispur and an awareness of what it meant to walk the corridors of power.

There were certain aspects of Jahnabi's girlhood that would give her the strength, in the coming future, to survive her ordeal.

There was absolutely no discrimination between boys and girls in her family. In many ways, it was a women-centric household, and many of them were well-educated and later very successful in their professions.

Next was a deeply ingrained faith in God, with prayers forming an integral part of daily life. From a very tender age, Jahnabi realized that she belonged to a family that enjoyed great respect and the goodwill of the people. They were *mouzadars* (an Assamese term to denote the head of a mouza, which is the subdivision of a district) who had a say in all matters related to community life. Her father and uncle were busy both in politics and business enterprises.

Jahnabi adored her handsome and dashing father Hiranya Goswami. She thought the world of him and took care not to hurt him in anyway. As a politician, he had a lot of charisma, and his young daughter noted with pride and admiration how he mingled effortlessly with everyone, without ever thinking of the barriers of religion, caste, or class. "I wanted to be like that, and most of all, I wanted to make my *deuta* (father) proud of me. I made up my mind that I would be a lawyer and defend the innocent. I also wanted to be a politician. "You must first get an education, girl," *deuta* would tell me, as "Only that will make everything else possible."

Then, out of a clear blue sky, came the bolt of lightning. In a matter of a few fleeting moments the world changed. Late one evening Hiranya Goswami left his home for some work. As a politician, he had been assigned security, but the guard was absent that day. In the darkness of Kampur, under a sky full of stars and amid fields of ripening crops, assailant pumped bullets into him, killing him instantly.

There is a pause. We can see Jahnabi's face quiver as she struggles to compose herself. I look down on my questionnaire, consumed by guilt at having forced her to relive some of the most traumatic moments of her life. Nandita sits on the carpet, her pen flying over the pages of her note book. I was suddenly reminded of those lines from the book *Rubaiyat* by Omar Khayyam:

The Moving Finger writes: and, having writ
Moves on, nor all your piety nor wit,
Shall lure it back to cancel half a line,
Nor all thy Tears wash out a Word of it.

Jahnabi gathers up the teacups and plates, bears them away on a tray, and comes back again. This little domestic chore seems to help, for she resumes talking.

At around midnight we had hundreds of people pouring into our courtyard. I had never seen so many people gather at one place before. The sight filled me with terror. And then, to know that in their midst was *deuta*, on the ground, under a white sheet, his body riddled with bullets . . . how could God be so cruel? It was as if the light had gone out of our home forever. Our rooms were filled with weeping mourners; I could not bear to see my mother's bare forehead. When *deuta* was taken away to be cremated the next day, hundreds of people followed his cortege for 8 to 9 km. The Bible and the Koran were read as priests chanted the mantras. For many of the villagers to whom he had given free land, he was like a father.

"This was in 1987. A few months later, my 85-year-old grandfather passed away. And at about the same time, my uncle, who had become our guardian, was diagnosed with cancer."

That pastoral idyll in which Jahnabi grew and played innocent pranks in the bosom of a large family was now a thing of the past. The dense bamboo thickets, the lonely paths between fields, the sight of strangers—everything seemed full of menace. Jahnabi and her family were now composed mainly of women, with only one uncle in residence and another living in Guwahati. There were days when the family was too afraid to venture outdoors. Jahnabi stopped going for dancing classes. There was nobody to go to the village grocer. Paranoia had set in and the shuttered house and its inmates seem to have come to a standstill.

Things were moving inexorably, pushing Jahnabi to her twilight destiny. First, the bullets of assassins felling her father, the patriarch. Then, the dreaded cancer ravaging her uncle. The dying man was filled with anguish. What was to become of his nieces and nephews, as well as his own daughter? There was only one answer. Eighteen-year-old Jahnabi had to be married off. She would have a home, a husband to take care of her, and she would have the chance to move away from that accursed home.

"I did not have a choice," says Jahnabi, her expression somber. "*deuta* was gone, Khura (parental uncle) was ailing. It was his last wish to see me as a bride. I didn't know what else to do."

So, Pankaj came into her life. Pankaj—handsome, well-off, and sophisticated. His father and Jahnabi's uncle were colleagues at the Food Corporation of India (FCI) office in Guwahati. After her first glimpse of Pankaj, Jahnabi forgot all her doubts about marrying. "I was totally smitten," she explains with a sad little smile. "The idea that this handsome boy from such a good family wanted me as his bride made me dizzy with happiness. All my friends envied me. In those days it never occurred to me that I should know him better. We met just three or four times, always with family members. I used to brag about him before my friends. I was very immature and all that mattered to me was he drove a car and smelt good."

Jahnabi's girlhood days came to an end with the smearing of turmeric on her body and the ululations of women as they carried sacred water in pots. It ended as exquisite gold jewelry and a gleaming *pat mekhela chador* (Assamese silk female attire) transformed her from a tomboy to a blushing, radiant bride, her collyrium-lined eyes searching for a glimpse of her groom. She sat by him before the sacred fire and the chants bound them for a new life ahead.

Jahnabi entered her husband's home in Guwahati. This was what she had dreamed of and waited, almost with impatience, fantasized, feeling at once bold and coy. But, from the very beginning, with the glow of turmeric still left on her skin, she felt something strangely amiss.

"Nobody came to see me, the new bride—no relatives, neighbors, or friends. I was never invited or taken anywhere. It was a bit disappointing, but I thought that perhaps my in-laws were very reserved people and maybe this was how people lived in the city."

"My life fell into a pattern. I would wake up, take a bath, wear nice clothes, put on make up. Then I would join Pankaj and his parents for breakfast. I was not expected to do any household work—there were enough servants for that. So all I had to do was deck out like a doll and idle time away."

"I got to know Pankaj better. He had a business dealing in cars and he also owned quarries. He was loving and kind to me but had a quick temper. There was a psychotic streak in him, and he was very suspicious. He did not like me to meet my male cousins. I found this stifling and quite abnormal. But I loved him and wanted to please him at any cost. So, I stopped talking to my friends and even family members just to please him."

But whatever Jahnabi did, it was never enough. For now, slowly, imperceptibly, her new family began to show their true colors. Her in-laws began to find fault with her, hurt her with cruel words, insulted her family. She was slapped, pushed around. There were bruises on her body, and a stunned Jahnabi woke up to the dark reality of an aborted dream. But who could she turn to for help? Her uncle, ravaged by cancer, must never know. It would kill him. Her mother, uncles, and aunts had problems of their own. Her sisters and brother were mere children. How could she add to their sorrow? So, Jahnabi found within her the strength to be a dumb doll, dressing in the way they expected a high-society daughter-in-law to do, and swallowing their jibes and insults. As the days passed, they prevented her from meeting her family and Jahnabi did not object, almost thankful for the exile as it would help her keep her dark secret to herself.

But there was more in store for the teenage bride. Pankaj, her Pankaj, was not well. She could never understand what really was wrong. Sometimes it was a splitting headache, or it was a fever.

Sometimes he lay in bed for hours, pale and listless. Or he would have loose motions. Once she was told he was having medicines for herpes. Nobody discussed with her what the matter was. His parents and sisters avoided coming to his bedside. Jahnabi noticed that Pankaj and she were served in utensils that were later washed and set apart. The funeral silence of the long days, her enforced idleness, the sight of her sickly and moody husband, it wore her out. So much so that when the family accused her of causing Pankaj to fall ill, she had nothing to say. It was as if she had lost the will to protest, to swear her innocence. Day-by-day the golden days of the past and the warmth and security of her maternal house seemed to grow incredibly distant, as if the memories themselves were fragments of a past life. As she sat by the bedside of her husband, she was appalled by his wasted frame and moved to pity by his strange suffering. He could have only a few spoonfuls of food at a time; looking at his gaunt face, Jahnabi was filled with foreboding. The walls of the accursed home, filled with cruel beings who hated her, seemed to have become a hellish tomb. Then, in the midst of these dark shadows, Jahnabi discovered that she was going to become a mother. Throwing up, feeling dizzy, and touching the growing mound of her belly, she see-sawed between elation and despair. Soon she would have another human being in her arms, flesh of her flesh, a boy or a girl, someone she would sing to, nurse at her breast, and play with. The little angel would certainly bring love, hope, and healing to them all. And yet, what would this child find in this home? A skeletal father, callous grandparents, vindictive aunt, and a mother subdued into silence. How could she take care of Pankaj and the baby at once? How could she cope?

Jahnabi gave birth to a baby girl at Kalicharan Das Hospital in Guwahati. The premature baby girl was delivered through caesarian section. Little Kasturi's paternal grandparents wasted no time in showing their indifference to her. Her father never clucked her chin or held her in his arms. She never figured much in his conversations.

Life for Jahnabi was moving to its swift, terrible climax. Soon after Kasturi was born, Pankaj fell seriously ill. He would cry out hoarsely from his bed, his ravaged body racked by pain. To Jahnabi's horror, the family members turned up the volume of the television set so that nobody could hear his screams from outside.

Still weak and bleeding after childbirth, Jahnabi made a decision. Pankaj would have to be shifted to a hospital. One night, calling one of her aunts for help, Jahnabi rushed Pankaj to the Guwahati Medical College Hospital (GMCH). All the medicines used by Pankaj had been regularly sent from Delhi, as they were not available in Guwahati.

"At GMCH the doctors did some tests. One day, a doctor took me aside and gently told me, 'Your husband is suffering from HIV/AIDS. Do you know about it?' I shook my head. I had never heard of the term. It was an illness and I supposed the doctors had a line of treatment ready for him. I said so to him."

"I'm sorry. There is no treatment for AIDS in India."

"That's alright," I said, "I'll take him to London then. My aunt stays there. I'm sure they have a cure."

"I was there in the hospital, nursing my baby, my husband slipping into unconsciousness or having psychotic rages, and all the doctors told me there was no treatment for AIDS anywhere in the world. It was then that it finally hit me. I would not be able to save the father of my baby. I was to soon become a widow, at 19. The world would end for me."

Then, in yet another twist to the macabre nightmare, a doctor simply told her, "Even you might have AIDS."

Jahnabi draws a deep breath and looks bleakly at me. I can sense that she is not in this cozy drawing room, with its sunset window view and snug sofas. She is in a hospital room with disinfectant smells, bottles of saline, gurneys wheeled along corridors, syringes, and rubber gloves, white-coated doctors, and a dying Pankaj. With her forefinger she touches a tear in the inner corner of her left eyes, as if plucking it away, stopping it from running down her cheek.

"When the doctor said even I might have it, I laughed and said, 'What are you saying? How can I have it?' It was then that Pankaj made me sit by him and listen. He told me how AIDS spreads, and admitted how he had got it from some woman during his carefree bachelor days in Mumbai. He had been suffering from AIDS for the last six or seven years."

"When it all sank in, I was stunned by how he had deceived me into marrying him. I was filled with rage by how he had destroyed my life. I looked him in the eye and told him, 'Do not ever think that I am going to spend the rest of my life being your widow.'"

"In his last effort to hurt me, he said, 'My parents are going to turn you out of the house the moment I die. Remember that.'"

"Pankaj fell ill at a time when there was no antiretroviral therapy (ART) available. In fact, even the doctors were full of apprehension about interacting with AIDS patients and would wear rubber gloves when handling them. My in-laws were filled with fear and shame about his illness. So they just stayed away from him. Nobody came to the hospital to see him." For almost three months Jahnabi tended to Pankaj in the general ward of GMCH. Nobody brought them food. Kasturi was often left at home in the care of a servant. "By now I had stopped applying *sindoor* (vermilion)," Jahnabi says. "I didn't have time to comb my hair for days. I took a relative's car to a beauty parlor in Chenikuthi and asked them to snip off my long hair, so that I did not have to comb it. I was in a daze, and no longer knew what I was doing. There would be times when I would sit by his bed, famished, exhausted, unable to sleep, to nurse my baby, and I would think 'When will he die? Oh God, when will he die?'"

There was nothing more that could be done. Pankaj was released from the hospital, to await his end at home.

It was the month of Bohag. The spring showers turned everything green. Cool breezes played with each new leaf and blade of grass. The streets were full of eager shoppers. Red and white woven *gamocha*s (hand woven towel) were displayed in makeshift stalls. In a quiet lane of Guwahati, Jahnabi, looking pale, with dark circles around her eyes, her hair cropped like a boy, stood by her husband as he gasped for breath and fell silent. This skeletal man, a being that seemed barely human, had been someone she had loved and desired and dreamt of living with happily ever after. And all she had was betrayal and cruelty. Jahnabi clasped little Kasturi and felt her life turn to ashes. It was April 6.

Fourteen days passed by. The funeral rituals were carried out. Then Jahnabi was bundled into the family car by her in-laws and taken to a private laboratory to get a blood test done. Then, without any explanation, she and Kasturi were turned out of the house.

Jahnabi returned to her parent's home, numb, broken in spirit. She had stopped talking. A year passed by in this manner, with Jahnabi spending time in her room all by herself, not doing anything, staring at the walls, and not interacting with her mother, sister, aunts, and cousins. It was as if she had retreated to a twilight zone, into a dense fog that muffled all sound, which simply swallowed her up. She became fearful and suspicious.

Two months after her return home, her family took her to a doctor in Guwahati who confirmed that she was HIV positive.

In those days there were no privacy policies to protect the identity of persons detected to be HIV positive and AIDS patients. She was probably the first middle-class woman in Guwahati to test positive. The names of all positive patients were published in newspapers, and when Jahnabi's name appeared in print, it marked the start of a long journey for this young widow, a journey of heartbreak and unexpected joys, galling defeat, and exhilarating victory. Destiny had many plans for her and a new life waited to be embraced.

***

All evening, people had been quietly filing into a new house at Sundarpur, just off the main Zoo Road. The walls have been freshly painted, the window frames still carrying the faint smell of

resin. There are about 15 plastic chairs in the front room. There
are girls in frocks and *salwar kameez* (north-Indian female attire),
hair neatly combed. There are mothers jiggling their restless,
drooling babies on their laps. An older woman in a white *chador*
(upper garment worn by females) sits with a lost expression on
her face. There are several men, well dressed, avoiding eye contact, and sitting patiently. One or two of them murmur among
themselves. It is difficult to know at first what binds this disparate
group together, till you see the banner strung across one wall of the
room. These are people living with HIV-positive (or full-blown
AIDS) men, women, and children who are here to celebrate the
29th International Aids Candle-light Day organized by Jahnabi's
Assam Network of Positive People and Assam State AIDS Control
Society (ASACS).

It appeared celebrating seemed to be the last thing on the minds
of the 11 women, three children, and eight men, shifting uneasily
in their seats. Jahnabi, who had made this meet possible, bustled
cheerfully among them, welcoming her guests, and overseeing the
arrangements. With her warm smile and cheerful, no-nonsense
manner, she succeeded in making these guests relax, and soon,
one-by-one, they open up before me. An elderly woman narrates
the traumatic end of her HIV positive son and the plight of his
young widow and her grandson. Almost everyone had similar tales
to narrate—how the stigma was killing more people than the virus
itself. Jahnabi has dedicated the premises as a care home for such
children in this house at Sundarpur, Guwahati.

At the gathering somebody asked Jahnabi if she considered
declaring her HIV positive status as an act of defiance. "I don't
think so," she answered candidly. "I had lost my husband, my child.
What else was there to lose? My coming out liberated me from the
shame and the burden of carrying such a dreadful secret. By telling
the whole world I was HIV positive, I got my courage back."

Jahnabi narrated how she managed to remain so upbeat about
life and the secret behind her tireless zeal.

"In the beginning I was filled with despair and stopped communicating completely. But my mother refused to let me sink into self-pity. She told me that I had to come out into the world to prevent my tragedy from happening to other women. The turning point came when I won a human rights case filed against the medical fraternity. The case registered had stated that an HIV patient should be kept along with other patients in a general ward and not in isolation as it is not an infectious disease. Hence, anyone could seek legal aid if faced with such discrimination."

"After I won the case, I was given two options—that of taking up a job or accepting a one-time compensation of ₹3 lakhs. My mother said if I took the money it would soon be spent, but a job would offer long-term security."

So Jahnabi began her new life as a receptionist in the ASACS, earning a modest salary of ₹2,500. Working also meant she had to relocate from Kampur to Guwahati. Initially she moved in with an aunt but soon wished to live on her own. She rented an apartment, little aware of the trouble awaiting her. The people at ASACS gave wide publicity to the fact that they had hired a HIV positive woman. Her landlord got wind of this and promptly asked her to leave. But that was not all. She was forced out of 13 houses by landlords who were horrified at the idea of her living in their premises. Perfectly normal sensible people became mean and downright hostile toward her. Traumatized, Jahnabi fled to her Kampur home, resolving to quit her job. She just could not take it anymore. But not for long. "Will you give up so easily? Go back, my child, and fight," her mother implored.

And what a fight it was. She came back to Guwahati, checking into a seedy hotel at Paltan Bazar, the commercial district of Guwahati, paying ₹120 per night for a tiny, airless room with musty walls and a sagging bed. She would leave the hotel, go to her office for the day, and return at sundown to sleep in that dark, miserable room. "These days at the hotel still haunt me," she says. I told J.C. Deori, the Project Director of ASACS, that I would have to give up my job as I had nowhere to stay. He arranged for me to stay at a room in the Training Center of the Health Department. This center was at an isolated place in the outskirts of Guwahati. Often she would be the only occupant in the large, deserted building, with only the *chowkidar* (security man) at the front gate. As it was not safe to go out after nightfall, Jahnabi would buy two *chapatti*s (Indian bread) and a *sabzi* (cooked vegetables) to carry to her room and have it for dinner. This was in 2002. She was on her own, left to her own resources, fighting to survive in a harsh world by her wits and the inspiring words of her mother. Two months passed by in this manner. Some city reporters got wind of her predicament, and suddenly there was wide media coverage. Jahnabi approached Chief Minister Tarun Gogoi for help, who allotted her a flat in the Housing Colony at Krishnanagar, Guwahati. It is here that we have come to meet Jahnabi. Till date, her neighbors have been very nice to her and quite circumspect about her HIV-positive status.

Meanwhile, there was much to aspire for and achieve. Once she had a home of her own, she threw herself into her job with renewed zeal. That same year J.V.R. Prasad, director general, National AIDS Control Society, came to Guwahati, and Jahnabi was the obvious mascot for ASACS. That seemed to pay off as Prasad, impressed by her tenacity and roused to compassion, ensured that she was promoted from a receptionist to a trainer, which fetched a hike in her salary as well. Soon Jahnabi was getting more involved in the struggle of millions as a member of the Indian Network of Positive People (INPP).

For a young woman who was once expected to dress up like a doll and have nothing to do and nowhere to go, Jahnabi has transformed into a powerhouse of energy, counseling patients, coordinating between different agencies, attending meetings, presiding over as President of the Indian Network for People living with HIV since December 2009. She had trained on planning for HIV/ AIDS communication and on clinical management and counseling.

She has traveled all over the world—to Thailand, Mauritius, Japan, Canada, Kenya, Mexico, New York, and Washington DC—to share her remarkable story with strangers, becoming one with them. All through this she has enriched herself with resource to work in her home-state through her organization, Assam Network of Positive People (ANP+), which was set up in 2002. They have succeeded in securing some facilities for HIV positive and AIDS patients, which includes free CDG count test, free travel for ART program, and free health check-up to all people living with HIV/AIDS (PLHIV).

She feels that women living with HIV/AIDS especially get a new deal. "Most of these infected women are very young. The married women didn't get support from their in-laws and are even rejected by their own parents. They face a lot of discrimination in society. I would say to every woman—go for a blood test before marriage. It is more important than matching the horoscopes of the bride and groom."

The purple dusk has turned into night. We are winding down this three-hour interview; Jahnabi has bared her heart to us, taken us through her life's darkest days, as also her moments of triumph. She remains unaffected by her status as an Indian icon and is quick to break into self-deprecating laughter. Pragmatic and disciplined, she has a brisk, no-nonsense manner that at times seems intimidating, until you realize that there is a scarred, vulnerable, and shy women behind that tough persona. She also loves cooking and trying out different recipes. As Jahnabi waves us a goodbye; you can't help feeling that she is just a bubbly, wholesome, girl next door.

2

The Only Man:
Monalisa Changkija

From the moment Tanya Chopra, all of 26, arrived at Dimapur from Delhi—Monalisa fussed over her like a mother hen. After all, many years ago, like Tanya, she too had been a young scribe, eager to step out of her comfort zone and do stories about forgotten and voiceless people. Tanya had been commissioned by a Delhi feminist magazine to write about how it was to live and work in the little-known Northeast of India. After some intensive research, Tanya had come up with a list of women to be interviewed and Tiamerenla Monalisa Changkija, editor, writer, poet, and feminist, was to be one of them.

"I want you to see the big picture," said Monalisa over tea and cookies at her home. "And I am going to first give you a view of Dimapur." So that afternoon, the two set off to walk the streets of the bustling town. They wandered among the ruined temples, monoliths, and baths of the last Kachari kingdom, which had existed before the 13th century. They then drove to the Diezephe craft village. Tanya exclaimed in pleasure at the sight of the cane, bamboo, and wooden artifacts, picking up a red and black Naga shawl for her mother. After lunch at a popular eatery, they visited the ancient village of Chumukedima and watched its waterfalls.

By dusk they were back at Monalisa's home where her daughters Tasungtetla Zeruiah and Yimjungpenla waited to greet Tanya. As the four of them chatted amiably, Monalisa turned to Tanya and said, "Are you game for a surprise?" "Oh Ma'am," Tanya said in protest. "I've given you enough trouble for one day. . . ."

"What . . . and go back to your hotel without tasting my Thevo Chu?"

"Thevo Chu," Tanya hesitated, "Come again?"

"That's pork with bamboo shoot!" said Yimjungpenla excitedly. "Its yummy, the way Mom makes it. You'll love it . . . you will."

"Wow!" said Tanya. "I'd love to."

Soon they were all in the kitchen because Tanya decided she wanted to also see how Thevo Chu was made. Monalisa briskly tied an apron to her waist, washed the pork, drained the water, and with a wickedly gleaming cleaver, chopped the flesh into 2-inch pieces. Lighting the gas stove, she put a pan over the flame and placed the pork on it, stirring it over in low heat. Daughter Tasungtetla had some chopped bamboo shoots ready, and as the pork started giving out water, she dropped the shoots into the pan. Meanwhile, the other girl had made a paste of ginger and garlic. While Monalisa added salt and red-chilly powder, Tasungtetla added the paste to the meat and continued stirring the dish. A delicious aroma of cooked pork filled the kitchen. Tanya trilled with pleasure. Soon, Monalisa's husband Ben joined them, and they had a lovely dinner of pork curry, steamed rice, and fried beans. Then Monalisa dropped Tanya at her hotel, with promise to meet the following day.

Back at her hotel room, Tanya changed into her sleeping suit, brushed her teeth, smeared her face with cold cream, and slipped between the sheets. On the bedside drawer was a small pile of books, magazines, and notepads. On top lay an article by the noted Gandhian Natwar Thakkar, whose Nagaland Peace Mission had worked for decades for the twin causes of peace and development in the state. She began to read.

Naga society is a tribal society consisting of 15 to 16 major Naga tribes. Each tribe has its own independent language, dress, customs, and manners. The practice of headhunting was at one time a vital aspect of the Naga way of life. It is no longer in vogue today, but it had been in practice till the 19th century. It is necessary to take note of this system, as it has been responsible in shaping the character of a Naga person as well as the Naga society. An important part of the Naga village administration was to cope with situations that might emerge as a result of a raid by a hostile village or vice versa. The practice of headhunting led to the cultivation of special traits of the Naga character. A Naga does not easily panic or lose nerve. The grooming of youth in warfare, tradition, history, social ceremonies, and songs and dances took place at the Morungs or youth dormitories. The Morungs also served as dormitories, but more than that, they were village academies to train the youth as soldier–farmers. The traditional system of self-governing villages has waned in modern times, leading to new problems.

The winds of change started blowing over Naga society with the creation of an independent district named as Naga Hills district and the advent of the first Christian missionaries of American Baptist denomination arrived toward the close of the 19th century. Then came the Second World War, during which the British fought a decisive battle against the Japanese in and around Kohima and drove them back. Yet another change with far-reaching implications for the Nagas was the transfer of power by the erstwhile British regime to the government of free India....

Tanya looked at her watch. It was midnight already. Somewhere from far away drifted the peal of a church bell. A car droned by. She put down the magazine on the bedside table, switched off the lamp, and pulled the blanket up to her chin.

It was only 9 a.m. in the morning, but Monalisa had plunged into work, talking on the phone, making notes for the next day's editorial, generally ensuring everything was in order. Tanya sat patiently in Monalisa's sitting room, waiting for a chance to speak. She had a good look at the woman before her. Stout and big boned, with a round face, pleasant in its plumpness, she looked slightly formidable, with a no-nonsense air about her. Sometimes her language was curt, staccato. And yet there was a genuine warmth in her, a spurt of generosity and openness, a kind of gruff tenderness that the younger woman found very appealing. At her magazine's office in Delhi, Tanya had researched extensively on Tiamerenla Monalisa Changkija, and what she had discovered was impressive. Born on March 2, 1960, at Jorhat, a major town in Upper Assam, Monalisa studied first at Jorhat and matriculated from Little Flower School, Kohima. An alumnus of the Patkai Christian College, Chumukedima. She graduated with honors in Political Science from Hindu College, Delhi, followed by a master's degree in the same subject from Delhi University. As she had done her MPhil semester on rural development, in the Department of Political Science, she came home to collect primary data for her thesis on analysis of rural development in Mokokchung district.

Her love for writing and the desire to play a proactive role among her people prompted her to pursue journalism, starting out as a columnist with the Dimapur-based weekly *Nagaland Times*, in 1985, with her widely read column titled, "The State of Affairs," and soon after, another column titled, "Of Roses and Thorns," in the Dimapur-based weekly *Ura Mail*, her work started appearing simultaneously in two rival papers based in the same town. She was also the first Naga journalist working as a correspondent for several newspapers and magazines outside the state. She has put herself in great personal risk in reporting the ground realities of a fractured society in siege.

Her anguish about the events unfolding in front of her and the fears and hopes of the common man yearning for peace found expression in powerful poems and short stories, all published in prominent national and regional newspapers and magazines. They encapsulated what could not be conveyed through dry statistics. Monalisa has published two collections of poems, *Weapons of Words on Pages of Pain* and *Monsoon Mourning*. One of her most powerful poems, *Not be dead*, was penned to honor the memory of Chahi Kevichusa, Editor of *Ura Mail*, who fell prey to assassins' bullets on September 23, 1992, and the protest was a brave stance for a woman who knew that she could well be the next victim. *Child of Cain*, with its Biblical connotation, was written after the twin bomb blasts in Dimapur's Hong Kong Market and railway station on October 2, 2004, wherein hundreds were killed and several more injured, including a group of children from a village of Kohima district, who were on an excursion to Dimapur, especially to visit the railway station, because they had never seen trains before. But it is not that Monalisa's ire is reserved for the insurgents with their AK 47s, who killed at will. She lashes out at the Indian Union, which made Nagaland a part of the nation, only acknowledging the existence of Nagaland in hyperbole and rhetoric. She resents how her people are clubbed into a category, as if earmarked for an anthropological study. Monalisa is the first Naga poet to be invited by the International Indigenous People's Forum to present her poems in 1997 at Oslo, Norway.

Monalisa is the only woman proprietor, publisher, and editor of a daily English newspaper, *Nagaland Page*, in the Northeast of India. A fellow of the National Foundation of India, she is the only member from the Northeast in the Planning Commission's National Steering Committee/Working Group on Women's Empowerment for the 11th Five-Year Plan. She is married to Bendangtoshi Longkumer, general manager, Nagaland Industrial Development Corporation. She is the mother of two daughters, Tasungtetla Zeruiah and Yimjungpenla Abigail.

"I'll be with you in a minute dear," Monalisa said apologetically. "Editing this paper takes a lot out of me. Do you see these photographs? They are three young men who vanished last month. Some say the army took them for questioning, others say they are being tortured by the militants for being police informers. But it is not just these three . . . all of us here in Nagaland are caught between the devil and the deep sea, and every day is a struggle to live normally."

"Ma'am, I read up a lot of academic papers on the Nagaland issue, and am no wiser for it. Can you give me a bird's eye view of it? After all, you have lived here most of your life, you have reported from the ground, and who better than you to clear my confusion."

"I am so glad you want to know," said Monalisa solemnly. "Time and again we face the insensitivity and ignorance of the mainlanders, and lose hope that we will ever be understood, much less given our due. So Tanya, here I go. You can take notes if you like."

Leaning back on her swivel chair, Monalisa steepled the fingers of her hands and began.

"You must first understand that the region has had a violent history, the seeds of which were sown even before independence. There are no less than 100 rebel groups in the Northeast with their own agendas for action. There have also been infighting among the states over the issues of ethnicity, resources, and inaccessibility. The unrest has led to low development. Denied of avenues of employment, frustrated youth are joining the rebels. All that the center comes up is ad hoc policies and lip service. That has given rise to feelings of alienation and distrust. Instead of ensuring our development, successive governments exploited our resources. Unable to find a way to empower ourselves, many of us took up guns. Some demand secession from the Indian Union, others call for autonomy or the right to self-determination."

Interjected Tanya, "I believe the Naga insurgency is half a century old."

"Yes, you're right." "It is not only the first but also the longest of secessionist turned insurgency movements in South Asia. The basic premise behind this struggle is the Naga's dream of a separate nation. Much harm was already done by the British colonial power, which considered their own economic and military advantage when administering the lands under their rule."

The telephone rang. Monalisa picked it up, issued short, staccato orders and hung up.

"Where was I?" she nodded her head. "Got it. You see, in 1946, a section of educated Naga youth protested against the merger of Naga territory with the Indian Union. The British were soon to leave India and a separate Naga state was what they felt to be their rightful due. They turned their Naga club into a political organization known as Naga National Council (NNC) which represented all Naga tribes. A nine-point agreement was signed between the NNC and the Indian Government in June 1947. The Indian Government was represented by Sri Akbar Hydari and so it was known as the Hydari Agreement. It laid down the point that there would be a review of the political status of the Naga hills after every 10 years. The Nagas believed that they would be free after the agreement's expiry. But as the Indian Constituent Assembly was planning to change the provisions of the Hydari Agreement, the NNC then turned to Mahatma Gandhi for help. He expressed the view that the Nagas should not be included in the Union against their wishes. But Jawaharlal Nehru pointed out that Nagaland was too small to stand by itself against two huge countries of India and China. So it was in its interests to be part of Assam and India. After partition, the Naga leaders insisted that as per clause nine of the Hydari Agreement, they had the right to freedom. The government was ready to only let the tribal minorities to establish autonomous district councils to help them have greater autonomy. At the head of the Naga Movement was the NNC leader Angami Zapu Phizo. Holding a plebiscite in Naga hills, which it seemed established that 99 percent of the populace wanted sovereignty, Phizo met Nehru in Delhi and put forward the demand for a sovereign Nagaland. Nehru's refusal led to the next phase; Phizo now brought together rival Naga tribes to create a nationalist entity with common goals. In this way there was a boycott of the first general election in the Naga hills. Phizo now formed a secret government known as Naga Federal Government (NFG) in 1954. Along with it, he raised a Naga federal army with 15,000 armed guerillas. When the Indian Army took up positions in Nagaland, Phizo flew to East Pakistan and later to London. When violence broke out in 1957, Nagaland was made into a single administrative unit. More trouble followed. The Indian government than made Nagaland an autonomous state within India under the external affairs ministry in 1960. On December 1, 1963, it was inaugurated as the 16th state of the Indian Union. But the separatists went ahead in trying to achieve nationhood as an independent and single administrative unit. In this unit all the Naga-inhabited areas of several Northeast states like Assam and Manipur would have to be included. After years of violence, ceasefire, and talks, the next milestone came in 1972, when the NNC was banned along with other militant outfits under Unlawful Activities (Prevention) Act. The rebel leaders finally sat in the negotiations table and signed the Shillong Accord on November 11, 1975. This agreement was to end hostilities between the government and the Naga factions. But the accord was rejected by hardcore NNC leaders like Isak Chishi Swu, T. Muivah, and K.K. Khaplang. They formed a new party. The National Socialist Council of Nagalim (NSCN) was formed in February 1980. Isak Chishi Swu, K.K. Khaplang, and T. Muivah were chairman, vice president, and general secretary, respectively.

The office peon came in with some papers, Monalisa scanned through them and returned them. "Get two coffees," she told him, and added, "One without sugar."

"So NSCN was keen to achieve a greater Nagaland. They stopped the violence and contacted other rebel outfits in the region. But ethnic divisions split the NSCN into two groups, one led by Isak and Muivah called NSCN (IM), and the other by Khaplang, called NSCN (K). Both the groups have continuously been at each other's throats, leaving behind a trail of death and destruction. Parallel governments are being run by no less than three groups, including one started by Phizo. Struggling to cope with this anarchy is the democratically elected government of the state.

"You see, a dialogue process started after a ceasefire agreement between the Indian Union and NSCN-IM leaders in 1997. Again in 2001, the Government of India also established a formal ceasefire with NSCN (K)."

"Assam, Manipur, Arunachal, and Myanmar erupted in protest when the Union Government talked of extending the ceasefire agreement to the Naga-inhabited areas of these three states and a foreign country. Such a step, they felt, was nothing short of acknowledging a greater Nagaland. So the factional conflicts continued, with no end in sight. There is confusion, uncertainty everywhere. Nobody is safe, and we have lived our lives in an endless state of siege. As if this is not enough, we have the army and paramilitary forces, armed with special powers, to tackle the insurgents. Innocent civilians are hauled off on suspicion. Many of them are not heard of again. The women are raped. Tanya, you cannot imagine what our people have gone through. That is why, in my own small way, I have dedicated my book of poems to those whom history ignored."

The coffee arrived, and Tanya switches off her recorder. Monalisa puts on her glasses and begins scribbling notes on the editorial that would have to be composed in an hour. Sipping her coffee, Tanya watches the older woman with quiet admiration.

Late in the afternoon, Monalisa takes Tanya to a popular Chinese restaurant nearby for lunch. It is crowded, with jazz music blaring away. They take a corner table, and Monalisa orders lamb Manchurian, hakka noodles, and talumein soup. A frugal eater, Tanya is only too happy to keep scribbling on her notebook between mouthfuls of food.

"You had once been described as the only man in Nagaland. What is your take on this? Were you flattered?"

"Name-calling is a common way to put down women in patriarchal society, if they follow their own way. I'm sure I've been called worse names. I take it as a compliment as my 'differentness' is at least recognized, acknowledged, even saluted. I certainly don't lose sleep over it. In fact, a long time ago, it was my own father who advised me that it's a man's world and so I have to learn the rules well and defeat men at their own game. Yes, being the proprietor, editor, and publisher of *Nagaland Page* is a success story. I am not raking in profits but am doing work that is fulfilling and useful to society. Again, after growing up in all kinds of God-forsaken outposts, in places without roads, studying under the light of kerosene lamps, carrying water in bamboo troughs, and my parents not being able to afford crayons for my artistic inclination—I have certainly come a long way. While I am proud of being a woman, I would prefer to be called a professional journalist or veteran journalist rather than a woman journalist."

"Can you share with me some of your life experiences in Nagaland during the peak of the Naga movement vis-à-vis the state security agencies?"

"Well," said Monalisa, wiping her lips with a paper napkin. "The state security forces in the 1980s till the mid-1990s were running amok and held the people to ransom. They fully used the Armed Forces Special Power Act (AFSPA), especially in districts such as Mon and Tuensang to take away people for questioning, torture them, and even snuff out innocent lives. I have myself undergone harrowing experiences at the hands of the security forces, particularly when I went to Mon district to cover the prime minister's, late Rajiv Gandhi, visit in 1987. The army at Mon questioned my intentions to visit Longwa, the Konyak village, through which the international boundary between India and Myanmar runs. They even destroyed a small bridge to prevent me from going there, and I had to walk the rest of the way. Even in Dimapur, when I wrote about the army's misbehavior, I was harassed. In Letters to the Editor, they questioned my morality, my credibility until the then head of GOC 3 Corp intervened. The army had the power to pick up anybody on trumped-up charges and hold them without producing them before a magistrate within 24 hours—sometimes they would even deny picking up anybody. But family members would approach me, and I would scream, rave, and rant until I was able to rescue quite a few people out of the army's clutches. Sadly, in those days there were no NGOs to do this kind of work."

"Let us talk about Merapani," said Tanya. "It seems your first-hand reports on the first Merapani War in June 1985 brought the public's attention to the role of women in such conflict situations. Again, your reports on the second Merapani War in 1991 established you as a courageous journalist who traveled conflict zones at night, unaccompanied and under the most adverse conditions. You told me earlier that the two Merapani wars were fought between police forces of Assam and Nagaland and are a part of the border disputes between the two neighboring states. Looking back, how do you view that experience."

"A war between the police forces of the states. . . ." Monalisa's face wore a bemused expression. "Perhaps it was the only such event in India? Those who came to know I was going to Merapani thought I had completely lost my mind, but then I don't believe in armchair journalism. I have to be physically present to get to the heart of the story. Mind you, it was more than a border skirmish— it was a serious struggle for control over a very fertile area. Borders in the Northeast had been drawn most arbitrarily, and conflict is inevitable because they threaten the traditional existence. Only by going there could I put context and perspective and explain the issue to the readers. If the journalists don't take risks, we have no business being in this profession."

Monalisa further entrenched her position as a committed journalist when in 1987 she traveled with her 11-month-old baby to Mon to cover Prime Minister Rajiv Gandhi's visit. At that time Mon district of Nagaland was practically under military rule, and the AFSPA, she recalled. "We traveled from Dimapur to Mon in a hired taxi, and my baby started vomiting throughout the 8-hour journey. Once we entered Mon district, we were stopped by the army every few kilometers and our luggage was checked. Each of my baby's nappies were taken out, and the feeding bottle was shaken, probably to ensure there were no bullets in it. Although the army men did not physically touch me or my baby, they would come very near, and I would cringe. It was very intimidating and my baby would shriek in fear every time we were stopped. In those days the media in Nagaland was totally sidelined, and the police chief even tried to prevent me from taking photos of Rajiv Gandhi's visit."

Monalisa faced many odds in her quest to file reports of the gross human rights violations and the many problems of the forgotten people of Nagalands' interiors.

Monalisa's trial by fire continued. A former MLA who could not stomach the fact that a woman could own, publish, and edit a newspaper, regularly took to faxing threat letters. More was to come. A citizen wrote his opinion in an article titled, "State is a reality and sovereignty is a myth," and requested that his name be withheld. Monalisa published the article sans the name. A certain insurgent group took umbrage and asked her to divulge the name. When she refused, they threatened her with dire consequences. Things came to such a point that the state government provided Monalisa with heavily armed body guards and house guards for an entire year. To this day Monalisa loyally stands by that unknown writer. She has never tried to strike any bargain with the insurgents because she does not want to jeopardize her credibility.

It is a warm summer evening. Monalisa and Tanya stroll along the streets of Dimapur, as dusk begins to fall. Monalisa is in the mood for more pleasant things to converse about. She begins, "In our childhood we were taught that the busiest person has time for everything. I do my own housework and also take out a daily newspaper. I have no maids to help me. Yes, I sweep and scrub my floors and my bathrooms, clear my dustbins, cook, wash, and iron clothes, ensure that no buttons are missing from my husband's shirts, the fridge is well-stocked, cupboards neatly kept, and I also write my seminar papers and editorials. I also manage to write poems, short stories, and articles. I even have my little rose garden and the lilies are ready to bloom. Last year I had a good crop of tomatoes. I am quite good at needlework and enjoy trekking to remote places. I enjoy playing carom and Chinese checkers with my husband and daughters. I don't enjoy cooking but can tackle Indian, Chinese, Continental, and Naga recipes. I cannot imagine a life of hectic parties, spending hours at the beauty parlor, and empty socializing."

Explaining how poetry comes to her, she says, "I don't brood over any subject, things just come to my mind and words flow from my heart. Since as a journalist I am in touch with everything that is happening around me, it makes me realize that everything in the world is interconnected. In this way the horizons are broadened. One's milieu and personal experiences play a big role in the creative process."

"The Poetry Society of India awarded you for your extraordinary contribution to poetry in Nagaland. How do you feel about that?" asked Tanya.

"I was thrilled but also humbled. Nothing feels as good as to be recognized and acknowledged by one's peers. But I must also say awards do not warmly embrace you when you go to bed at night. My greatest inspiration is interacting with people and empathizing with them. Any literary work that is distanced from the reality of the people is like Naga pork curry without salt."

They laugh and turn around a corner. Cars and bikes drive by. The street lights came on and people throng the shops.

"Tell me, Monalisa," Tanya enquires teasingly. "What makes you angry?"

"So many things and so many people," she says with a rueful smile. "Most of all, people who assume and presume too much and too many things about you. There are those who claim to know everything about me, whereas I am only discovering myself."

"And where do you get your courage from?"

"From God, from my parents, from my experience, and exposures to so many things that have happened—particularly from my experience of having to stand up, struggle, and strive for what I believe in. I was brought up to fear nothing and nobody. So I guess I just grew up being a person for whom fear is a stranger."

"How proud are you to be a Naga?" asks Tanya. "How important is identity to you?"

"It's very important. Identity means many things to me, and I also look at identity as very plural, because, you see, I have my identity as a woman, a Naga, a wife, a mother, a journalist, a poet, a daughter. . . . Identity is something I look at that enables and empowers me to be much more than a Naga or a woman or just this and that. This is what is so enjoyable about living in these modern days—one can be so many things at the same time."

"What do you think would happen if we women were to rule the world?"

She is quick with her reply, "Oh, the world will be a better and happier place to live in. We wouldn't be busy trampling on one another just so we can stand up, be counted, suppress, oppress, and dominate others. And yes, the world would be more tolerant, more understanding, more appreciative, and more forgiving."

They were nearing Tanya's hotel, "There's just one more question. Can you describe a typical day in your life?"

"I don't actually have a typical day, though I try to have one. I get up late, do my household chores, work at my computer—I work from home, preparing the next day's edition."

"In between, there are a hundreds of social and family obligations, then my creative writing and reading. I love doing crossword puzzles and watching movies. During seminar season I am busy preparing papers. I don't have a proper eating and sleeping schedule. I am often overworked, exhausted, and tensed up. For you see, I not only do the editorials but also the inside pages—news, post-eds, and op-eds etc. I'm fully hands-on as far as my newspaper is concerned."

It is time for the two women to part. Tanya impulsively hugs the older woman and says, "It was wonderful to meet you Maam. I have learnt such a lot in these few days. I will mail you the interview when it appears next month."

"I'm glad you came," says Monalisa warmly. "You gave me a chance to go over my life. And you have all the makings of a first-rate journalist. Have a good trip, dear."

In the light of the warm summer evening, Monalisa walks home, her mind already on the work waiting for her.

3

Born Free:
Parbati Barua

I am about to meet a woman—elusive, mysterious, and a living legend—known as perhaps the only female mahout (a person who rides an elephant) in the world. Books have been written on her, films have captured her daring exploits, and her life has been one long love affair with the gentle beast. She has spent years among them, talking to them, feeding them, bathing them in the river, issuing commands, even singing to them. I have wanted to meet this larger-than-life character, this splendid, brave, and free spirit of womanhood for years. And then, amazingly, I discover that she lives with her sister when in Guwahati, only a short distance from my home. On a muggy monsoon evening, with frogs croaking in the dense and dripping undergrowth, I unlatch her gate, and I am at once greeted by the furious barking of a dog inside. The pet having been safely tied up, Parbati Barua answers the door herself. Slim and of medium height, she holds herself very erect. Her frame is spare, angular, and her bespectacled face looks at me with some wariness. I introduce myself and she ushers me in. The living room is a large hall with a coffee-brown upholstered sofa set, a sideboard filled with tiny knick knacks and large framed photographs of her father, Prakritish Barua, also known as Lalji, of the royal family of Gauripur, and her older sister, the celebrated singer of Goalpariya folk songs, Pratima Barua Pandey. I explain how I want to travel deep into her life and reveal to readers the amazing world she has inhabited. I wish to take her through the years she has spent loving and caring for the great beast. She listens, her hands folded on her lap. She is wearing a crisp cotton sari. Her hair is tied back in a severe bun. Her dark eyes behind those glinting spectacles are watchful, giving away nothing. It is tough-going for me, more so because the room is dark, lit up only by a small bulb placed over an aquarium. Even the fish darting around in the greenish water seem a little sinister. I try out a spur-of-the-moment ploy, a desperate gambit to win over this somewhat unlikely prima donna.

"I'm so glad you left the room dark," I say ingratiatingly. "It makes it much easier to imagine a forest, doesn't it?"

That does it. A smile appears on that wintry visage. She becomes a little more animated, opening up, revealing how she would rather read a book than listen to silly women gossiping, how most of her days are spent traveling, and how she has rice three times a day without fail. By the time my visit comes to an end, Parbati Barua has given her tacit approval for the project, but she warns me that I am not to dig into controversies. I promise to provide her a questionnaire at the earliest.

There is a catch, though. My background research on this legend would remain flimsy without a thorough reading of Mark Shand, the British author of *Travels on My Elephant, River Dog*, and other books, as a BBC conservationist and travel writer, authored *Queen of the Elephants*, which was published in 1995, and the corresponding BBC documentary of the same title released in the same year. The book is a modern classic on Indian wildlife, combining Kiplingesque ambience with Durrellesque humor. *Queen of the Elephants* won the Thomas Cook Travel Book of the Year Award in 1998. But returning to the catch, this book is nowhere to be found by My Girl Friday, Nandita. She and I ransack all the book stores in the city and contacted umpteen book-loving friends. The irony is, Parbati Barua grimly holds onto her own copy, refusing to part with it even for a couple of days. Weeks pass by and then, finally, there is a glimmer of light. Journalist Roopam Barua, related to Parbati, not only has the book but is cheerfully willing to lend it, that too without a time limit. Better still, he has a vast knowledge of Parbati's life in the wilderness and gives me access to extensive published material on her, most of which he had himself penned. I finish the book in a few days, totally riveted by Parbati and her daring exploits. Mark and Parbati journey through the jungles of Assam and West Bengal, along the foothills of Bhutan, finally resting on the banks of the Brahmaputra, just in time for Magh Bihu, the auspicious harvest festival. Goalpariya folk music fill the air as Pratima Pandey joins them, singing songs of hopes and aspirations of the humble rural folk—farmers, boatmen, mahouts, and artisans. Parbati shares the wealth of her knowledge about the great beast with Mark. The pair shares their concerns for its future. Besides the journeys along the forests, there are trips to the magnificent Mal Bazar elephant squad and to Parbati's ancestral home—the Motiabagh palace. One of Parbati's most famous quotes is strikingly graphic. "It is not from books that you learn about these animals. It is from here—she struck her forehead and then slapped the left side of her chest—and from here."

When you learn of Parbati's life in the jungles, which makes her vulnerable to the elements, the heat of the summer sun to the biting cold of winter, pelting rain, and fog, and the attendant troubles—living with the most basic of amenities and subjecting the body to cruel privations—you feel a great respect for her, more so because of the fact that she was born the daughter of a zamindar and could have led a life of indolence, even extravagance, filling her days with frivolous amusements. To understand her, you have to know where she comes from.

The history of Gauripur's zamindar family finds ample mention in the noted historian and sociologist Nagendranath Basu's three-volume work, *The Social History of Kamrup*. According to him, Parbati's paternal grandfather, Raja Prabhat Chandra Barua, was the adopted son of Pratap Chandra Barua, who belonged to the lineage of Govinda Bhuyan. It was in 1856 that Pratap Chandra Barua settled in Gauripur, moving in from Rangamati. Her maternal grandmother, Sarojbala, followed the Vaishnava faith of the Saint Sankaradeva. The ideals of love and compassion for all living beings can be traced to her. Returning from Delhi after attending Lord Curzon's Delhi Durbar, Sarojbala discovered that she was pregnant. Pramathesh Barua was born on October 3, 1903. Four other children followed—Niharbala, Nilima, Prakritish, and Pranakesh. Pramathesh Barua immersed himself in amateur dramatics from a very early age, starting the Gauripur Young Men's Association (GYMA) club in Gauripur. He staged plays like *Chandragupta*, *Europe*, and *Rani*, directing, acting, arranging music, and lighting for them. He had a pet elephant called Jungabahadur and was a skilled and fearless hunter. He shot an astonishing 52 Royal Bengal tigers, besides cheetahs, bears, deer, wild buffaloes, rhinos, and birds. After his education at Presidency College, Calcutta, Pramathesh Barua moved to the world of cinema. He learned modern techniques of movie lighting in Europe. He made a silent film *Aparadhi* in 1930 and produced it himself. That same year, he was elected to the Assam Bidhan Parishad. He successfully produced several films, including the magnum opus *Devdas*.

Pramathesh Barua's brother Prakritish Barua was renowned the world over for his legendary expertise and knowledge on elephants.

The family history dates back to the 8th century. Sometime in the 15th century Narahari Rai, one of their ancestors, who was a minister at the royal court of Mithila, came back to Kamrup after an altercation with the king and was installed as an administrator in the royal court of Cooch Behar. In 1620 Mughal Emperor Jahangir gave the title of king to Kabi Shekhar, a descendent of Narahari Rai.

Gauripur lies in a forgotten corner of India, a small town on the western side of the district headquarter, Dhubri. The Gadadhar flows gently by the main town on its eastern flanks. There is a lake on the northwest named Laokhowa beel and on the northeast, by the river bank, is a small hilltop called Motiabagh on which the Hawakhana palace is located. This is where Parbati's life began.

"Do you know the story of how Gauripur got its name?" she asks me on her next visit. "My ancestor Raja Pratap Chandra Barua was the zamindar of Rangamati. One day, he went out to the forest to hunt. There he saw a frog swallowing a snake. It was an unusual sight and he believed it was a supernatural sign. He was a devotee of Goddess Mahamaya. He then built a temple in the name of the Goddess and named the place as Gauri, Gauri being one of the names of Maa Durga."

"I was named Parbati, the mother of Ganesh, the elephant-headed God. When I was only 1 month and 17 days old, our father broke journey from Shillong to Gauripur and halted at an elephant camp in Damra. That was only the beginning. All through our childhood years, father took us to stay in these camps, seven to eight months a year. We all went along—my father had four wives, we took with us 70 servants, including cooks, a doctor, a barber, and a tailor. A tutor accompanied us so that our studies were not interrupted. We lived with these gentle giants and their handlers in a kind of paradise. We rose at dawn and helped in preparing fodder for the elephants. We keenly observed all the activities at the camp. Well-trained elephants called Kunkies (koonkies) drove away wild rogue elephants and this saved the villagers. The men in the camp shifted troublesome wild elephants to other areas to avoid overcrowding, tamed elephants to uproot lantana creepers, and removed fallen trees on the roads. The elephants were even lent to timber merchants for logging operations. My father loved elephants more than his life, and he paid close attention to every aspect of their well-being, including massages, bathing in the river, treating of ailments, and their diet. They were fed green gram, digestive mixtures, herbal potions, salt, jaggery, besides plantain and grass. We saw how the handlers trained new elephants with treats and light taps on the legs and head to make them understand the instructions. The leg chain, bedi or collar, and the neck chain were tested to see that the elephants were not hurt. In the evenings, we would sit with father and the mahouts. There would be long discussions on matters related to the camp. We were expected to listen attentively and pick up tips. Many wonderful stories about elephants were also narrated. In this way nature became our university, and I, its most ardent pupil."

And that she certainly was. As a toddler, she experienced her first adrenaline rush on being able to make a tame elephant move by standing on its head. Riding behind her father, she went hunting in the forests. A wild boar suddenly shot under the elephants' belly and escaped to the other side. The elephant jolted in panic, and Parbati went off flying to the nearest thicket. Lalji calmly proceeded to go after the boar. Her father's matter-of-fact reaction signaled to the young girl that though she was bruised and every bone of her body ached, she was not to be a crybaby. And little Parbati bravely pursed her lips and kept quiet.

It was no surprise, therefore, that at age 14, she caught her first wild adult tusker. How could a mere child achieve this? "Catching an elephant is not a matter of brute strength," she explained. "It's all in the mind and some amount of luck." She caught this pachyderm in the Kachugaon forests in Kokrajhar district. Till date she treasures the two words her father joyfully uttered after her brave feat, "Shabbash beti!"

That was only the beginning. Parbati chose to live and work in the midst of her beloved elephant family. It takes a lot of patience, perseverance, and dedication to tame elephants. Catching a wild elephant is an extremely risky job. They are captured by throwing a lasso around their heads. The process of training is very slow. It takes about six months of gentle coaxing to win the beast over. Parbati's three pachyderm daughters are Lakshmimala, Aloka, and Kanchanmala. The trio and a team of coworkers lead an unusual and adventurous life. Different states like Bihar, West Bengal, and Assam request her help in tackling rogue tuskers or tend to those who are injured/ailing. She is consulted on elephant management policies, in controlling capturing wild herds, driving out wild herds from urban areas, and training mahouts. "In my job, there are no retakes," she states grimly. "Every time I go to the forests, I think of it as my last trip. But as a mahout, I can never retire."

When she is not working, Parbati loves to dress up decorously in *mekhela chador* (Assamese female attire) or sari. But the time for action sees her radically transformed. She is then togged out in faded jeans, combat jacket with shiny brass buttons, a solar topee, and sunglasses to shield her eyes. Tucked in her waistband is a *khukri*. She even chews a bit of tobacco. Appearance is important for her beloved pachyderms too. She tenderly decorates their foreheads with chalk. Going by her attire, it is not hard to discern that Parbati is a die-hard fan of westerns. Her heroes are rugged men like Charles Bronson and John Wayne. She also loves to watch war movies. Her favorite movies are *The Magnificent Seven, High Noon,* and *How the West Was Won.* Her life in the wild is bereft of modern conveniences. She uses ash instead of toothpaste, sleeps inside a tent, on a threadbare mattress, that too without any pillows. She keeps by her bedside a sepia-tinted photo of her father Lalji in his youth. And all around her are ropes, chains, *khukri*s (a sharp knife), stirrups—the tools of her trade.

"There are many rituals in our work," she explains. "These have been handed down for generations. Every journey begins with a puja to Goddess Kali, Ganesh, Saatshikari—the patron goddess of forests and Muslim saint Mahout Pir."

I told her I am curious to know about the mela shikar. Parbati's eyes glint with excitement. "It used to be an elaborate affair. First, a camp would be set up in the jungle. Then the men would scatter all around to watch the movements of elephant herds. All food items were carried on bamboo tubes or sacks. We did not carry any metal, so as to avoid noise. When we were out to catch elephants, the mahouts and *phandi*s (elephant catcher) even smeared themselves with elephant dung and urine. Elephants are short-sighted and hardly look up. Usually we chose smaller elephants to catch. The *phandi*, seated on a tame elephant, throws the lasso over the wild elephant's head. It requires perfect timing and great skill and balance. It has to be isolated from the herd and led back to the camp for training. After training, they are sold to merchants and zamindars as well as royal families. My father supplied elephants to the royal families of Bhutan and Cooch Behar."

In her early years, from 1975 to 1978, Parbati's area of work covered western Assam, North Bengal, Jalpaiguri, and Darjeeling. The West Bengal government sought her help in 1980. She caught and trained no less than 12 elephants. A dramatic incident took place in 1987–1988. A herd of wild elephants moved from Dalma forest in Bihar to the wilds of West Bengal. They did this every year and returned after grazing. However, human population had begun to increase and panicking due to the shouts of villagers, the herd lost its way and wandered about disoriented in the forest. In this way they crossed Kangsabati River and entered the jungles of Medinipur. They wandered among the sal and eucalyptus forests, gave birth to calves, and became restless as winter ended. They attacked nearby villages and three people were killed. There was widespread terror. Forest personnel were unable to take the herd back to Dalma. At that time Parbati used to rent out her own trained elephants to the West Bengal Wildlife Department. The government requested her help. Parbati, seated on her elephant, led the herd back to their home in Dalma, achieving in two weeks what the forest department had failed for three months. This amazing feat led to media frenzy, and she became an international icon. The grateful villagers bestowed on her the title of Hati Devi. BBC made a film on her titled, *Jungle Jumboorie*. She was honored in 1989 for welfare and management of both wild and captive elephants. The Government of Assam conferred on her Honorary Chief Elephant Warden of Assam for her lifetime achievements. Mark Shand wrote not only a marvelous book but also an eponymous film for Discovery Channel. She is the only woman elephant catcher and practioner of mela shikar in Asia and, probably, the world.

Parbati returns to the person who had shaped her for this destiny. "I hero-worship my father and owe everything to him. He felt he was far from society, in tune with the ways of the wild. He discovered wisdom in animals. He was an MLA, but his heart was not in it. He was a widely traveled and sophisticated man but chose a very different life. He loved his elephant Pratap Singh so much that when it died, he stabbed himself in grief. There is a stone mausoleum of Pratap Singh in the grounds of Motiabagh palace. Instead of living in the lap of luxury, he chose to be a *mahaldar*—catcher and seller of elephants, courting danger at every step, roaming freely under an open sky."

Parbati, however, has had her share of brickbats, along with the bouquets. In 2003, Green Oscar award winner Mike Pandey captured on film the torture inflicted on a young elephant caught by Parbati in Chhattisgarh. The elephant died after 18 days and the footage was widely screened for the media. This created a big furor. "The elephant was declared a rogue before the Chhattisgarh government called me to tackle it," she says impatiently. "Rogue elephants are dangerous and of course they have to be tied with ropes. The film avoids showing how we tried to take care of the animal after we caught it. Isn't this selective filming?" That was not all. A few years later Parbati was again in the eye of a storm, when the animal rights group, People for the Ethical Treatment of Animals (PETA), and Maneka Gandhi's People for Animals raised a hue and cry over the alleged torture of elephants during preparations for the just-concluded centenary celebrations of the Kaziranga National Park. Parbati had trained elephants for an exhibition football match, but it was abruptly cancelled. "People make an issue over nothing just for publicity," she says. "Can they love elephants more than one who has spent her entire life among elephants? Have they seen elephants carrying tourists in 45°C heat in Delhi and Jaipur, how they are made to walk over hot melting tar on the roads?"

India is home of between 50 percent and 60 percent of all of Asia's wild elephants and about 20 percent of the domesticated elephants. Wild elephants are facing many problems, most of which pertain to habitat loss and man–elephant conflict. Population explosion and clearing of forests for development have posed problems for these giant beasts. With this in mind, the Government of India initiated Project Elephant in 1992. Its aim was to preserve their habitat and establish elephant corridors, in order to maintain the traditional migration patterns of the elephants. Resolving man–elephant conflict issues and taking note of domestic elephants were also a part of its agenda. The project presided over the establishment of 25 elephant reserves and covered an area of 58,000 km. It has also established the Monitoring of Illegal Killing of Elephants (MIKE) program of Convention on International Trade in Endangered Species of wild flora and fauna (CITES). There has been a significant increase in poaching of bull tuskers for ivory and this has led to an imbalance in the sex ratio.

Domestic elephants have their own set of problems. Maintaining an elephant is an expensive affair. Many owners and mahouts exploit the public reverence for the animals by using them to beg in the streets. Prevailing conditions for upkeep of elephants in the cities are deplorable. Elephants used for tourist rides are overworked and underfed. There are rules to protect these animals, but they are rarely enforced.

Little is discussed about the economic aspects of the Barua family's bond with elephants. Tim McGirk of *The Independent* has it that the Baruas paid annual taxes to the Mughals in the form of six war elephants. But after India's independence, the State stripped the maharajas and princes of their wealth and land. A great blow was struck with the abolition of the privy purses in 1970, which greatly reduced the wealth and power of royal families who bought elephants from the Baruas. Lalji was then owner of the Motiabagh palace and a stable of 40 elephants. How would he maintain them? His solution lay in the forests that had sheltered him. Together with his fearless and resourceful daughter, he got into the business of capturing wild elephants, taming them, and selling them to private parties or the Sonapur fair. But even this came to an end in 1977, when the Indian government banned the capture of elephants for commercial purpose. The ailing and impoverished Lalji, a shadow of his former self, did not live long. Parbati took part in the funeral rites and then vanished to the jungle to grieve alone, with only her elephants for company.

Fortunately, not long after, she found a purpose in life—to mediate in the man–elephant conflict. In India's countryside, hundreds of wild elephants were killed by angry villagers into whose territory they strayed. They were also hunted for ivory. As she says, "My work was to rescue man from the elephants and to keep the elephants safe from man. All the elephant wants is peace and safety. If a man is killed millions are there to replace him. But if just one elephant is killed, the species draws closer to extinction."

Elephants, pushed against the wall by the reduced green cover, poaching, man's aggression, are starting to attack humans more frequently. This has been validated by S. Deb Roy, former Conservator of Assam's forests. Previously solitary bulls attacked humans but now females are also easily enraged. As many as 200 Indians are killed by elephants each year, and most incidents take place in West Bengal's Jalpaiguri district where they are hemmed in by rice fields, tea gardens, and villages. This is where Parbati has had to intervene with her knowledge and expertise most frequently. Elephants that kill without provocation are declared rogues. But it is found that even rogues have some injuries inflicted by man to cause it to go berserk. Parbati and her elephants are then called to coax these beasts back to the jungle.

For a long time Parbati has lived in a modest house near Subansiri tea estate on the Bhutan foothills, renting out her elephants. She has been married twice, first to a banker, but life within the four walls is clearly not far her. Her first marriage, to a man chosen by her father, lasted barely a year, and even Lalji had to concede there was no future in it. Instead of cooking, embroidery, and tending to children, she craves for the heart-thumping, pulse-racing moments of pitting her wits against the wild elephants she struggles to tame. In those moments, she even forgets her name. Instead of the normal 30, she can make the beasts obey 42 commands. She has in-depth knowledge of the herbs elephants find for themselves when they are sick or wounded. She loves to sing soulful love songs to soothe her beloved beasts.

What does Parbati feel about her belonging to the zamindar family of Gauripur? What was it like growing up in a palace? Surely her childhood was exotic? "We children never felt we were privileged. It was the people around us who put us on a pedestal. Our parents gave us freedom instead of luxury. We were encouraged to mix and get along with all sorts of people. However, befitting our station, we were waited on hand and foot. Our every need was anticipated by those tending to us. However, my father, who was a scout and had even gone abroad for a jamboree, dinned into us the importance of being self-sufficient."

"As a little girl I hated playing with dolls; I found it a very boring pastime. I liked to play outdoor games and hang around among the elephants and horses. During the rainy season, we would have great fun running around the vast wooden verandah of Motiabagh palace." She describes to me the ornate balustrades of wrought iron; the gallery of trophy heads; her father's Sanskrit texts, diaries, and notebooks; and the framed pictures of hunting expeditions. The palace reverberated with music. Bejeweled *khukri*s glittered on walls. Outside, the elephants rumbled.

"It was not that suddenly one day I decided to become a mahout. Tending to elephants was something I had done from a very tender age. My father and other mahouts had passed all their wisdom and experience to me. Because I was educated—I have a graduate degree from Handique Girls College, Guwahati—I was able to process this in a rational way. For example, we were told to avoid doing some things on moonless nights or full moon nights. I learnt from books about lunar influence. Emotionally too, I was geared for this life; I was happiest in the company of these beasts. I understood their generosity, their nobility and loyalty. Humans cannot match up to them. It is true that sometimes elephants kill man, but only when they are provoked. Let me tell you a story. A herd of elephants suddenly appeared before some villagers working in the fields. Screaming in alarm, the villagers ran away. A woman even abandoned her own baby. And do you know what happened? One of the elephants gently picked up the baby with its trunk and took it to the village, placing it on the front porch of a house.

Parbati has spent a lifetime among elephant-catchers, also known as *phandis*. But their fate causes her to feel despondent. The once thriving art of elephant capture met with a sudden death following the inclusion of the elephant in the Scheduled List of Species in 1977 under the Wildlife Protection Act, 1972. Deprived of their livelihood, these men have been reduced to abject penury. Equally significant, their expertise in this art will soon be lost in oblivion.

Parbati intimately knows the kind of life they have led and feels deeply their despair. Doing that kind of work calls for tremendous courage and nerves of steel. As she says, "Every time I enter a jungle, I think it will be the last time around. And that my death is round the corner. An encounter with a rogue elephant and the attempt to put it on the leash is a gamble between life and death. An elephant can understand 40–50 commands. But to make them obey, one has to have a full grasp of their psychology and deal with their extraordinary intelligence and memory. One must also have the stamina to handle their strength. If you can do all this, sitting on elephant back is as safe as sitting in your bedroom."

This is a woman who has had a life unlike that of any other. Her fame as the first female mahout in recent recorded history has traveled much beyond the shores of her native country. Today Parbati lives in Guwahati with her sister in a spacious home in the shadow of the Sarania Hill. She often travels to destinations she does not disclose. She is shy, even awkward, in company. She leads a spartan life. She dreams of the bejeweled midnight sky over some vast, whispering forest, the hoot of the owl, and the soft rumbling sounds of her beloved elephants. It is a world that is vanishing fast and the sadness of that realization is clear in her dark eyes.

4

Silencing the Whispers: Birubala Rabha

Darkness had long fallen over the hills, forests, and fields surrounding the village of Thakurvila in Goalpara, on the Assam–Meghalaya border. The cattle had been led to their sheds, and the women had cooked supper over smoky wood fires. The men had sat in their courtyards, wrapped in coarse shawls, smoking *bidis* (Indian cigarette), and talking about the harvest to come. Then, one by one, the huts fell dark as families retired for the night. Only one woman was awake. And as the curs howled at the sickle moon that hung from a starry sky, Birubala Rabha quietly slipped out of her house, a silent shadow. She walked swiftly, almost running, lifting her *dokhona* (Bodo female attire) up to her ankles, her brow furrowed. The bamboo copse creaked and shivered as she crossed it, and an owl hooted from its depths. She moved past fields, climbing hillocks, wading across shallow streams, panting with exertion, knowing how each moment counted and how on her depended the life of another.

She had known Sunila Rabha for five years. Sunila had come as a bride to the next village, setting up home with Bireswar, a poor wage-earner. Something about Sunila's shy, trusting nature and easy smile had endeared her to Birubala. They often met in the weekly market, where Sunila sat behind neat heaps of fresh carrots, tomatoes, and greens grown on her tiny plot of land. Her three-year-old Sumbi played by her side. The two women talked of flower designs that they were planning to weave, the difficulty in getting kerosene from the fair price shop, and the fishing festival they would all take part in, wading into the river, tossing the nets, pulling in the catch.

Then, unknown to them, a dark cloud hovered over young Sunila. There were whispers about her in the village. Men and women stood talking in low, urgent voices, throwing malevolent glances in her direction. They stopped talking to her or buying her greens. Sunila was puzzled, hurt, and then alarmed. What had she done? What were they saying about her? Then, on his way home from work, Bireswar was stopped by a village elder.

"Son, we have nothing against you. But this cannot go on. Every man, women, and child is in danger. Your neighbor Sonaram's girl is dying. The *ojha* cannot cure her fever. It is unlike any illness we have seen around here. Your woman is the evil one, the *daini* (witch). She has cast a spell on the poor girl. Tomorrow we will meet at the *Gaonbura*'s house. Bring your woman there; the villagers will decide what is to be done."

Without losing a moment Bireswar cycled to Thakurvila, his mouth dry and heart racing. He had to save the life of his gentle, sweet-natured Sunila. What madness had gripped his people to suspect her as a witch . . . Sunila, who would never utter a harsh word to anyone?

Two hours later, he was at Birubala Rabha's house. "Help us, sister," he pleaded. "Only you can save her. They are meeting tonight and have asked me to take her there."

He covered his face with his hands, weeping, kneeling down in front of Birubala. She passed her hand gently over his head and made her promise. "Your wife is a good woman. Go home, Bireswar. I will do what I have to."

By now Birubala had been walking for two hours. Beads of sweat stood on her brow. On a nearby hill side, foxes had started their eerie howling. Far across the paddy field, she saw a bright orange glow, rising above the tops of betel-nut trees. Birubala stared at it for a moment and felt her heart grow heavy with sorrow. It was her worst fear to come true. She could not keep her promise to Bireswar. That was his house that the villagers had set fire. By now she was running across the field, stumbling, falling, picking herself up. Then she was in the midst of a restless crowd gathered around Sunila. The young woman lay sprawled on the ground, her clothes torn away from her, her arms crossing her bare breasts. She was keening like a wild bird caught in a trap. The people took turns to pull her long hair, kick and pummel her soft body, spit on her. Thirty feet away, the ramshackle hut that had been the couple's home was up in flames. Birubala took in the scene and a while hot rage coursed through her. She had seen this macabre drama played out in village after village, all through her life. It was bad enough that they were poor and unlettered and helpless in the face of disease and starvation. It was bad enough that the marvels of modern life were denied to them. But what were these beliefs that brought out the devil in them, which made them prey on their neighbor with such hatred and cruelty?

Birubala pushed through the crowd to where Sunila lay on the ground. She took off her worn shawl and covered the almost unconscious woman, cradling her in her arms, murmuring words of consolation.

"What are you doing, woman?" demanded a village elder. "She must die. We have found out she is a *daini*."

"Enough!" Birubala's voice cracked like a whip. Then she began to speak.

***

The history of witch-hunting goes back far into time and is as old as the hills. In Europe, thousands of innocent men, women, and children were burnt at the stake by the public in the Middle Ages, suspecting them of casting evil spells.

In India, countless instances of witch-hunting have been reported from Rajasthan, Gujarat, West Bengal, Bihar, Maharashtra, Andhra Pradesh, Jharkhand, and Orissa. A report says 2,556 women were killed across the country between 1987 and 2003. Bihar alone registered 522 cases of witch-hunt between 1991 and 2000.

In Assam and the Northeast, such beliefs continue to prevail in this 21st century, and gory murders of hapless women often take up newspaper space. Mayong in Morigaon district was once known as the citadel of black magic in Assam and people came from faraway places to master the dark arts. Assamese folk tales are replete with stories of grisly human sacrifices and macabre practices. Even today belief in witchcraft is widespread among many communities and tribes all across the Brahmaputra valley. Ojas (a traditional medicine man) or bez (exorcist) are those who master the black arts and are treated with awe and fear. Interestingly, such ojas are supposed to have ghost servants called beera (poltergeist) who do all their mischief for them. There has been a disturbing upward trend in witch-hunting in Assam over the years. A staggering number of 500 lives have been lost and 116 official cases of witch-hunting have been registered in the past five years. But few cases are resolved, mainly due to the lack of witnesses.

In this day and age of revolutionary technological progress, spread of education, dissemination of information, it seems incredible that people could still hold on to such superstitions. But in a region torn apart by insurgency and besieged by floods, backwardness, poverty, and disease, the blessings of modernity have passed people by. This very vulnerability is taken advantage of by quacks and, even more dangerously, by people who have an axe to grind. Lack of access to modern health care means that people try to treat cholera, malaria and so on through medicines prepared by ojas, who all too often are quacks. When the patient is unable to recover, these medicine-men are at risk of being beaten up and even killed. So they are quick to lay the blame at somebody's door. A new trend of using witch-hunting as a means of grabbing land belonging to the victim has also been noticed. Rampant alcoholism among the rural populace also triggers irrational and irresponsible behavior.

Witch-hunt cases were reported in recent years from Kokrajhar, Udalguri, and Sonitpur districts. It is also widespread in Kamrup (rural), Goalpara, Chirang, Baksa, Lakhimpur, and Karbi Anglong districts. It is practiced by Bodos, Rabhas, Mishings, and the tea tribe community. Illiteracy is rampant, and lack of roads and bridges makes these places inaccessible. There is no health care, schools, sanitation, or potable water. Entire families have been chased from their homes, stoned to death, chopped into pieces, and even buried alive. Groups of people, often entire villages, act in unison, thus ensuring that no one reports to the law-enforcing agencies.

***

On that moonlit night, surrounded by a ring of hostile faces, Birubala held Sunila against her breast and began to speak.

"Shame on you!" she cried, pointing a finger. "Can you see her now? If she is a witch, why does she bleed? Why has she lost her senses? You fool, Sunila is one of you. She feels the hunger that you do. She feels the cold, the heat, sadness, and joy. Look at her clothes. Are they not shabby like yours? Look at her house . . . you turned it to ashes. But what was it? A hut of cane and straw, with a mud floor. Why did she not use her power for a better life? Why did she not go to a better place instead of being poor and hungry here? Did the *oja* tell you she is a *daini*? Do you believe everything that he tells you? Then you are no better than sheep. Use your reason."

"Listen to what happened to me. My 15-year-old son Dharmeswar became mad. He kept wandering here and there, acted strangely, even beat me up. I did not know what to do. So I went to the *deodhani* (Deodhani), the medicine man far away, to make my son sane again. Do you know what the *deodhani* said to me? 'Birubala, there is no hope for your son. He has married a fairy and the fairy is with child. When that child is born, your son will die in three days. There is nothing more to do.'"

She drew a deep breath and continued. "My son did not die. He is alive, in a place far from here. The *deodhani* was wrong. And I lost faith in all the mumbo jumbo. And do you know what the villagers wanted for my poor mad son? Death. They wanted to kill him. I sent him far away and he lives there still."

The crowd melted away. A woman came forward with a rag and a bowl of water to wash Sunila's wounds. Her husband and child came to her, weeping. Birubala gathered her shawl around her and began her long trek to the village.

Hailing from a poor family, wife of a farmer in remote Thakurvila of Goalpara district, bordering Meghalaya, little about Birubala's earlier life explained her emergence as a gutsy crusader well beyond middle age. Orphaned at the age of six years, Birubala tackled domestic chores and homework with her trademark diligence but could study only up to Class V. She, however, more than made up for that with her skills in cooking, embroidery, weaving, poultry rearing, and other useful activities. By the time she was 16, she was setting up her new life with husband Chandreswar Rabha and quickly became the mother of three sons and a daughter— Dharmeswar, the oldest, followed by Bishnu Prabhat, and the youngest son, Doyalu and daughter Kumoli. Life was tough and they had just enough to keep body and soul together. The even tenor of their quiet lives was interrupted when the eldest son, Dharmeswar, then 15 years of age, began to change. He muttered to himself, stayed away from home for days, feared imaginary foes, and even hit his mother. In desperation, his father visited an *oja* for help. The *oja* had an explanation that was stranger than Dharmeswar's ailment. It seems that the boy had married a fairy who was going to be the mother of his child. As soon as the baby was born, the *oja* warned, Dharmeswar's life on earth would end. Dharmeswar would live for just three more days. The little household waited for death, already grieving for poor Dharmeswar. Days came and went, and the boy remained alive. Birubala's fear turned to relief and then, indignation. How dare the *oja* make such wrong predictions? With her innate sense of justice and fair-play, Birubala realized that other villagers, her community, needed to be taught about the importance of being reasonable, shedding superstitions, and breaking free from the stranglehold of wily medicine-men who preyed on their fears, ignorance, and helplessness.

Inheriting a love for social work from her mother Sagarbala, Birubala formed the Thakurvila Mahila Samiti. It was from this platform that she raised public awareness against witch-hunting and other social ills. Then she became the secretary of the Greater Borjhara Mahila Samiti. In 1999, she became a member of the Assam Mahila Samata Society. Soon, as she spoke passionately in more and more meetings, it became a rousing cry against the darkness of ignorance and shackles of tradition. That was not all. At great personal risk, she saved 35 people, both men and women, from certain death at the hands of hostile villagers who had accused them of causing illness, death, or some misfortune. She sheltered another victim in her own home and narrowly escaped being killed herself. Slowly, over two decades, the story of Birubala and her gutsy crusade began to be reported by the media. She became the talking point among the chattering classes. Feminists were eager to call her one of their own. The simple woman, clad in her handwoven clothes, looking thin, wiry, and outspoken, became the poster girl of a new campaign for change and modernity. Awards started to pour in. In September 2012, social activists launched Project Birubala, a novel mission to reach out to witch-hunt victims and bring about changes in the outlook of communities cut off from modernity. The mission has been launched in Goalpara and Kamrup at present, but plans are afoot to spread the campaign to other districts. Birubala emphasizes that merely saving victims is not enough and the victims must be repatriated with their families or given shelter and taught a livelihood. Assam Police, through its innovative Project Prahari, initiated by IPS officer Sri Kula Saikia, has joined hands with the State Women's Commission to activate community policy against witch-hunting. The commission has prepared and submitted to the government a draft law on witch-hunting, so that a strong law can be used against offenders, just as it is being done in Bihar and Jharkhand.

Both Birubala and Assam Mahila Samata Society, an NGO, have been fortunate to work with each other. While the society found in her a tireless crusader with access to the masses in Assam's remote countryside, Birubala felt a sense of belonging in becoming its member, and the organization was able to intervene in many sensitive cases that came to her knowledge.

The Assam State Women's Commission has made certain recommendations. There must be trauma counseling and retreat shelters for victims. Provisions must be made for women's court at *panchayat* (village courts) level or village development council level. There is a pressing need to enact laws to ban witch-hunting. A state policy to root out this social evil must be formulated. Adequate study of customary laws and sensitization on this issue has also been recommended.

What is the tripping point when a simple villager becomes a source of evil, a witch? "Every village has an *oja*, a medicine man and astrologer. He is the one who reads our fortunes," begins Birubala earnestly. "And if he mentions someone as a witch, everybody believes him. There is another way people find out about a witch. If a villager falls ill and no medicine seems to work, he is covered from head to toe with a net. People then prod his body with sharp sticks. He screams and cries in agony, but the villagers want him or her to name the evil one. Very often, just to escape these attacks, the poor person utters someone's name, calling him or her a witch."

"What happens then?" I asked. She explained: "The woman named as a witch will be ordered to appear before the whole village. Her crime is related to her and she is either chased away or trapped in a net and tortured by prodding with the sharp point of a spear. When such a woman is killed, her body is hacked to pieces and buried in separate places to prevent her rebirth. When such a person is chased away or killed, the land and other assets are seized from them. Family members are often too terror-struck to object, in case they meet with the same fate."

Witch-hunting cannot just be dismissed as a social evil in a backward region. It is a flagrant violation of human rights. According to Mamoni Saikia, District Program Coordinator, Assam Mahila Samata Society, Goalpara, "In Assam several women's groups spearheaded by Assam Mahila Samata Society (AMSS) have now turned their attention to the problem of witch-hunting. We have been pressing for a law or policy to bring an end to this practice. The greatest problem we face when uncovering such instances is the lack of witnesses. Everyone is afraid of antagonizing the majority. And how are we to give protection to witnesses if they come forward?"

In Assam's remote countryside, a region cut off from progress and development, people live in a time warp. Ignorant, unlettered, and poor, they are easy victims of quacks and people who want to settle personal scores. The so-called witches are isolated, displaced, tortured, and robbed of belongings. Social boycott and forced regulation lead to tragic suicides. Married women branded as witches are abandoned by husbands, who marry again. Families break up and mothers are separated from their children. There is loss not only of property but also of livelihood. Children of alleged witches drop out of school. Displaced women and children are at risk of falling into the hands of human traffickers.

Bihar was the first state in India to pass the prevention of Witch (*dayan*) Practices Act of 1999. Jharkhand followed with an Anti Witchcraft Act in 2001 along with the 2005/2006 Chandigarh and Rajasthan laws. Shockingly, there is no such law in Assam. Except for a Project Prahari by Assam Police, there is no legal measure to punish offenders.

Life has come a long way for Birubala. In 2005, the Northeast Network nominated her for the Nobel Peace Prize. That same year, she was felicitated by Reliance Industries Limited in Mumbai under their third edition of Real Heroes—ordinary people, extraordinary service—and she has found mention in Switzerland's 1,000 Women Peace Project, which has honored 1,000 female peace workers from ISO countries around the world.

In 1985, she became the secretary of the Thakurvilla Mahila Samiti, and she moved from village to village in rain or shine, speaking out against these barbarous practices, winning admiration, making enemies, scolding, persuading, inspiring, holding out hope to victims, and arousing fear in the perpetrators. Then she was made the secretary of the greater Borjhara Mahila Samiti in 1991. In 2006, she began her association with the Assam Mahila Samata Society. At this time, she had begun to speak out against rape, kidnappings, and dowry-related cases as well.

In spite of all the honor and adulation heaped on this feisty woman, her life remains simple, even harsh. The day before she came to meet me in Guwahati from her village, she had worked the whole day at a road-repairing site under National Rural Employment Guarantee Act (NREGA) with her job card. Some city-based organizations invite her to speak or to honor her, and all that is given to her is the bus fare. Birubala, of course, is too proud to open up about her needs, and the stories of her privation remain cloaked in silence. Rather than being disheartened by her poverty, she continues to dream of her pet project, a shelter home for victims of witch-hunts, where doctors would help them cope with trauma of torture, a place where they would be safe, fed, clothed, taught a trade, given the courage to fight back, and reclaim a dignified life.

In 2000 Birubala attended a meeting organized by the AMSS to raise awareness about witch-hunting and its evils. Women from several villages flocked to the gathering, and the society activists began by asking the gathering, "Do you believe in witches?" There was pin-drop silence. The woman looked at one another. No, they were not going to say something that would get them in trouble with the menfolk later. In fact, hadn't they all had to take permission from their husbands to come here? Then, suddenly, Birubala stood up and spoke out in a clear, loud voice. "I do not believe in witches. There are no witches, only people believe they are so." The women huddled together and refused to echo Birubala. She then spoke about her son and how the *oja*'s prophecy was false. There was an uneasy murmur among the crowd. "The men and women we chase away or kill are our brothers and sisters," she stated. She asked, "Who gives us the right to destroy their lives?" The AMSS at once warmed up to Birubala. Here was a simple village woman with a message that would strike at the very heart of this vexed issue. They saw in her the spark with which to bring about a transformation. But Birubala was to pay dearly for her crusading zeal. Barely three days later, she was summoned to a meeting by the village elders of Thakurvila. She was attacked with a barrage of questions: What had she said at the meeting? Who did she think she was? Why was she trying to be their enemy? Why had she said there are no witches? Who had given her the right to speak on their behalf? Cruel words of abuse were hurled at her. The whole village had turned up, each man and woman ready to thrash her with bamboo poles. She was ordered to sign a piece of paper taking back the words she uttered at the meet. She would not only have to acknowledge the presence of witches in the community but also support the people's decision to root them out. Birubala's mouth hardened into a thin line. She stood there head unbowed, staring straight at the enraged crowd, refusing to take back her words and sign the paper. Then she was removed from the post of secretary of the Thakurvila Village Samiti, the body she had herself created. All the registers and seals were taken away from her. Then the village decided to boycott her for three years. Nobody was to visit her home and fines would be imposed on anyone who dared to break this rule. Birubala listened to all this, taking it all in, defiant, unrelenting. For the next couple of years the villagers shunned her and her family. Birubala continued her work, this time as secretary of the Borjhara Mahila Samiti. Now her canvas was much larger. Besides raising awareness on this evil, she developed contacts with the police and the district administration, lobbying for good roads, potable water, health care, education, and funds for development works. She was her usual blunt self before top government functionaries, including the Deputy Commissioner, and she was very often the catalyst of change in the way things functioned.

In a twist of fate, it was not long before the villagers of Thakurvila changed their attitude toward her. Over the long years of insurgency, many village youth were hauled off for questioning by the police and the army. Many were arrested on suspicion of being terrorists. Countless families spent sleepless nights wondering how to get their loved ones back home. It was at this juncture they figured things out. Birubala had valuable contacts with the police. Perhaps she could help? Swallowing their pride, they desperately appealed to her for help. Birubala was not one to hold a grudge. Besides, precious young lives were at stake. So she promptly strode off to the nearest police station and said, "Eh, why have you taken so and so into custody? I have known him since he played on his mother's lap. He is no terrorist. Release him at once." Such was Birubala's integrity that very often the police took her on her word and grateful families welcomed their sons back. The tide had turned for Birubala. The villagers who had humiliated and shunned her now embraced her as one of their own and a savior who brought light into their lives.

This plain-speaking women with the dust of country roads on her feet, her hair tied back in a tight bun, her hands calloused by years of hard labor, sat before me in her best *dokhona*, green and yellow with gold threads running through it, one that she had woven at her own loom. She waited patiently for my questions and allowed associates, a young Krishak activist, and Usha, her relative, to answer many of the questions. She spoke forcefully and artlessly, making frequent hand gestures. All through the meeting, she held a magazine covered with old, yellowing newspaper. It was the strangest magazine I have ever got my hands on—a book of witches. Brought out by the Assam Mahila Samata Society, it contained photographs and stories of the hapless women targeted as witches in villages spread across lower Assam, Jonali Rabha, Sabitri Hajowari, Lauchon Rabha, Anita Rabha, Khedai Bala Rabha, Charonia Rabha, and each had a harrowing tale to narrate. Many of them owed their lives to Birubala. But this savior has no time to look back on her success and the many triumphs of her two-decade-long crusade. Because she knows that every day, somewhere far away, in some sleepy hamlet lost in time, someone is being singled out for that midnight knock. And she, Birubala, would have to stop the wheel of fate.

5

Walking Tall: Urmee Mazumdar

It was close to midnight when I clicked to clinch my friendship with Urmee Mazumdar (I never use her formal name Suchismita) on Facebook. She lives barely 10 minutes away from my home, and we have met on and off for close to two decades. Our conversations over the years have ranged from our children, our jobs, to our spouses. I even remember a particularly spooky ghost story she related one afternoon when she dropped into our Assam Tribune office to hand over some press release. Urmee is petite, small-boned, with beautiful dark eyes looking out of a chiseled face that almost always wears a solemn expression. Her voice is low and musical, with a throaty inflection that sort of gets to you. She had long hair once, but now she sports a stylish bob that gives her a girlish, pixie look. There is something very relaxing about Urmee's presence. It is as if she accepts you as you are, as if she is in no hurry to go anywhere, and I have to say this, she has never badmouthed anyone in all the years I have known her.

But how much do we know a person? Don't we often assume we know them well, only to discover after some incident that they are utter strangers? I have to get to know Urmee better because I have to write about her, get under her skin, reveal her brave struggle against a crippling disability, but I don't want a cardboard cut-out

of a poster girl of the "differently abled" (the terms keep changing faster than you can remember). So here come the Facebook
pictures: Urmee at a table, in a russet *kurta* and funky blue-framed
glasses. Daughter Pakhi captions it, "My backbone! My *Ma*."
There is a heart-shaped cake and a gleaming candle, marking the
first wedding anniversary after the passing away of Urmee's husband Binoy. Mother–daughter duo share a great love for praline
chocolates, carrot cake with cream, and Urmee writes, "It's my life
and yours, live and let live, all will be happy in the end."

On the evening I go to meet her and sound her out on the
idea of featuring her in this book, Urmee is in bed, even though
it is only early evening. She has had a nasty fall and fractured her
already weak leg. Propped up by large pillows, her leg in a cast
right up to her thigh, she gives me a rueful smile and describes the
incident with a shrug of her delicate shoulders. Her mother is in
the room, to keep company. Urmee has books and files all around
her, and the laptop close by. She cannot be still for a moment and
in the soft glow of the bedside lamp, she is like an elfin trying to
get away.

"I couldn't have chosen a worse time to fracture my leg,"
she grumbles. "There's my daughter's wedding coming up. I've
had the caterers over to decide the menu. Pakhi wants it to be
just right. And then the trousseau, I must get the *mekhela chadors*
from Sualkuchi." She glances at her husband Benoy's photograph
framed on a side table.

"He left us so soon . . . and I have to do all this alone." A
shadow flits across her face, but soon she is urging me to partake
of some sizzling hot home-made snacks and cups of cinnamon-
flavored tea. She listens to my book proposal, nodding, her face
alive with anticipation. Of course she would share with me her
life's story—struggling against great odds, endlessly overcoming
her limitations, putting on a brave face, challenging fate, and finally
inspiring and helping others like her.

Pakhi's wedding, at the sprawling Gymkhana Club in Guwahati, is a glittering affair. As the guests mingle and congratulate the couple, there is admiration for Urmee, the single mother, who has overcome her bereavement and the accident to make sure that everything is just right.

Finally, she has time to turn back the pages of her life's book and go back to the very beginning.

"I am the eldest of the four siblings who grew up in a pretty house called Reff House, which belonged to my father, late Kripa Nath Dutta and mother Smt Mondira Dutta. The house stood on a tiny hillock on Kench's Trace, beyond Laban, in Shillong. My two younger brothers, Partha and Siddhartha (Geetartha was yet to be born), went to Sishu Mandir School in Bishnupur. I missed a year due to my illness, and so my brother Partha, the older one, and I were in the same class. It was an English-medium school, and our friendly Bogi Miss, the headmistress, was a kind woman who made us feel wonderful. I was average in my lessons but loved to recite nursery rhymes with action, as taught by our head teacher. My brothers and I were the best buddies. We had the same friends in our neighborhood, and after school we got together for some fun. Because I could not walk properly, my brothers and friends thoughtfully included me in playing marbles, crawling games, *gilly danda* (a game), ludo, hide and seek, and acting out drama skits. I was never sidelined and made to feel sorry for myself. Nobody commented on my handicap. Maybe that is the reason why I have always believed myself to be equal to everybody else and not claimed any privileges."

"When did your parents seek medical help for you?" I ask.

"Well," she continues. "I was just one and a half years old when I suffered from a persistent high fever for several days. The homeopathic medicines could arrest the fever for a few hours and the onset thereafter scared my parents. They contacted my mother's relative, Dr Bhubaneswar Barua, who asked them to bring me immediately to Guwahati. The doctor was shocked to discover that I had polio, a rare disease at that time, and the vaccine for it had not been introduced in our country. By the time the treatment started, the right side of my body was already losing all sensation. The doctor stationed himself at my grandfather's house at Jorpukhuri and for three days and nights pushed injections one after the other to arrest total paralysis of the right side of my body. After a long ordeal, he could save only the upper part of the body and the upper limbs. The whole of the right lower limb was totally paralyzed. My family was devastated. But my parents were practical enough to start me on physiotherapy and messages once we got back to Shillong."

"Then, when I turned 13 my father told me that an orthopedic surgeon from England, Dr Bolin Gogoi, was coming to Guwahati to help children with polio by performing corrective surgery on them. We had just migrated to Guwahati after shifting of the Assam capital due to the creation of Meghalaya as a separate state. My brother and I went to St. Mary's Convent. We lived in the new house my father built at Silpukhuri. Father's words gave me some hope. I was beginning to tire of walking to and from school with my right leg dragging after me."

"When I met Dr Gogoi with my parents, I begged him to make my leg strong, so that I could walk for miles and miles without tiring. 'Don't worry,' he told me cheerfully, 'you will be able to run around and even play lawn tennis if you like.' Finally, the three-phase surgery started at Guwahati Medical College. Dr Gogoi conducted muscle transplantation from inner thigh to knee, strengthened my calf muscles, and tended to the feet tendons. I was in hospital for six months and never complained for a second. There were visitors throughout the day and my brother brought so many Junior Classic comics that they piled up and became a side table at my bedside. Since the hospital was located in Pan Bazar, a commercial place, I could ask for coca-cola and ice-cream at any time. Seeing me treated like a queen, with my every wish being fulfilled, my youngest brother Gitu said he wished he too had polio like me. We all had a big laugh over that. After some tough physiotherapy, I was finally released from the hospital. I still had a limp, but my leg was stronger and I could run. Back home, my carelessness caused fresh trouble. I walked over a plank on a rain-filled read and slipped, twisting my operated knee. The pain was excruciating, and my parents were furious that I had not been more careful. My father called up the doctor, who assured us that there was no fracture, but that only a bit of the surgery had come undone. I was asked to rest for 21 days before a final assessment could be made. As a result of this I could walk but was unable to run. So, no lawn tennis for me. But I did not brood for long. I had learnt to accept whatever I got in life and my needs were very simple."

"So how was it to feel you were different from others?"

"My youngest brother arrived soon after my recovery from Polio and I had a companion to play with. My mother was busy with him so I was looked after by my father and an *ayah* (maid). When I was four years old, I realized something was amiss, because whereas my younger brother could walk around to get his toys, I could barely stand without support. I was his older sister, his ba, but it was he who was walking, while I was crawling. My other brothers also did the same. There were times when I threw tantrums because it was so frustrating to be like that. But by and by, my brothers gathered around me to listen to my stories. They, my cousins, and friends involved me in all their games, and I felt loved and needed. I would often bruise my knees by trying to run like them, and it bothered me a lot. My parents told me it was a dreadful disease but that I would get better when I grew older."

"Sometimes my brothers would initiate my walk, and my father would explain how we were all different, with different traits and abilities: 'See, Partha is so fat he can hardly climb trees, whereas

Siddhartha has a sharp nose to sniff out trouble, and Gitartha was so thin and dark as a baby. How different you all are. It doesn't matter how Urmee walks, as long as the job is done. Is that clear?'"

"So what if I could not run? In the years to come, my brothers and I were as thick as thieves, getting rid of a tutor whose teaching we did not like. We bunked guitar classes on Sundays to go to morning shows. I used to compose letters for Partha to give to his girlfriends. Partha in turn would bring letters addressed to me from his friend Binoy (who later became my husband). Binoy came to me one day with an enormous pair of goggles. He shyly told me he did not know how to talk to a girl but that he wanted to be my boyfriend. I had this big jolly gang of brothers and cousins and did not much care for an exclusive relationship. "Let's be just friends," I suggested. So in many ways, I was enjoying a normal life and had the vanity of a normal teenager. I was very proud of my waist-long hair and threatened to stop going to school if my father cropped it in a pageboy style."

"In the 1970s and 1980s, any form of disability was seen as a curse. Families would be torn apart with shame and wallow in self-pity. People would gossip and give unsolicited advice. A child had to endure the double burden of his or her handicap and guilt about the suffering he or she is causing to the family. Often the mother was the one who was blamed for the affliction. Things were, of course, much worse in the villages. The disabled person was often neglected and subject to emotional abuse because he or she was not a productive member of the family. That was not all. They were often lodged in barns and outhouses and served meals there, as if they were animals. No wonder, many of them could not survive for long. The discrimination and abuse stemmed from the fact that a disabled person could not earn an income. That is why, as a disability activist, I lay stress on skills training for disabled youths above 18 years. There have been instances when young women have deliberately chosen to marry disabled youth because they are skilled artisans and earning a comfortable income through their micro-enterprises."

"As a young girl, I had to listen to an aunt stating bluntly that I would never be able to get married because no boy would propose to me. Later I found out that only two percent of people with disabilities (PWDs) were able to lead a conjugal life. Even my in-laws made discreet enquiries before the wedding if my illness would be passed onto our children. My enraged father almost called off the wedding."

"But things are much better today, thanks to the United Nations Convention on the Rights of Persons With Disabilities (UNCRPD) Act for recognizing the fundamental rights of persons with disabilities and ratification of the act by many countries, including India. The Government of India, slumbering with the People With Disabilities (PWD) Act, was finally asked to implement the UNCRPD in all the departments of the government, by which the disability sector has gained access to all welfare schemes. Persons with disabilities now have equal rights to education, health, livelihood, and social recognition for their individual achievements. It is a slow process but, nevertheless, it is happening, thanks to the social activists, NGOs, and general well-wishers all over the world."

Urmee pauses and takes a sip from a glass of water by her table. "You must understand that a big milestone was achieved by the UNCRPD, which so many countries ratified, and this law demands equal fundamental rights for these marginalized citizens. The fallout of UNCRPD is great for us, as it has also the penal obligation which binds everyone toward non-discrimination of disabled persons at all levels. This convention focuses more on children with disabilities, women with disabilities and severe or multiple disabilities. The PWD Act 1995 did not have this panel component, and hence, its implementation by the government was nil."

"Let's get back to you." I suggested gently. "Do you lapse into self-pity? Or is it true that you push yourself in order to prove you can in fact achieve more than people without disabilities?"

"My upbringing has been such that there has been no room for self-pity. Like my father, I understood the value of developing a work culture. After my graduation with English honors, father set about preparing to enroll me in postgraduate classes, but I put my foot down, as I was determined to find a job and become independent. Further, I did not want to do my MA, as I knew I could not shine academically. I could write the answers very slowly and so had to leave the answer scripts incomplete. I also did not much fancy a lecturers' job, which was often the only option for Arts graduates those days. My dear friends Ashok and Rubi Barpujari then arranged for me to appear for an interview held by the Divisional Manager of Usha International (then Usha Sales Limited) and I came out in flying colors. I joined as a Commercial Assistant in Usha with a six-month in-service training period. So armed with a diary, I entered the corporate world, jotting down indents, invoices, and delivery of fans, sewing machines, diesel pumps, and piston rings to Usha dealers all over the Northeast. Slowly I made myself so indispensable that my boss depended on me for the smallest details at the public and coordination department. He, Mr Bindra, often praised me and coaxed me to join the Usha Sales Ltd. office at Ernakulam. I was proud and happy when I got my first salary. I promptly bought a tape-recorder and offered my parents to pay the wages of our cook Raghu and meet other expenses. I felt really proud when they agreed. But this lasted for only two years. In 1981, I got married and moved to remote tea estate in High Range Munnar, Pullivasal, where Binoy worked for Tata Tea Ltd. I became just a housewife, and all I had to do was to cook and keep our home spic and span. But then, unknown to me, my shift from the corporate to the social welfare field would begin from there. The ladies of High Range offered me an honorary job of looking after the crèches and rehabilitation work in the tea estates. Once again I was back in action and loving it. Binoy was also very proud when I gave my feedback to all the Senior Managers every Saturday at the High Range club. The people there were very curious to know about the headhunters, the practice of paying bride price, and even the reason why we had mongoloid features. I answered them as best as I could and they were entranced by the *mekhela chador*s I wore to the club meets. One day some tea pickers even asked me how many buffalos Binoy sir got to marry a poor, disabled girl like me. I stretched my hands and replied, 'Lots, he got lots.' When the manager heard about it, he wanted to reprimand the women, but I pacified him, saying it would take years to sensitize them about disability. I was also learning Tamil and my interactions with the laborers helped me pick it up more easily."

"Then I got pregnant and my parents were over the moon. In fact my father wept when I first told him on the phone. I came back to Guwahati and was spoilt rotten. I had always been 47 kgs and now I gained 10 kgs. My mother cooked me delicious meals, and I polished off everything double quick. My mother-in-law sent me cream and *rasagolla*s from North Lakhimpur, and my father-in-law sent a huge rahu fish every now and then. My mother-in-law came once and not only slept by my side, but woke me up early morning for a walk. I hated getting out of bed, but the walks helped me to remain fit. Finally, on the auspicious day of Bijoya Dashami—on October 19, 1982, my son was born. As I held his tiny body in my arms, I realized that I was indeed blessed."

But Urmee had more, so much more to give to the world. Being a wife, and then a mother, was simply not enough for her. There was a spark in her that made her want to push her limits. This time she had in-service training at Sishu Sarothi, the Institute of Cerebral Palsy, Assam, and after a series of training programs outside Assam, she earned a license as a Rehabilitation Personnel from the Rehabilitation Council of India, New Delhi. With the help of her sister-in-law, Arzoo Dutta, she had the good fortune of meeting social activist, late Sanjay Ghosh, who briefed her on the process of starting work on disability in the rural areas where there was a crying need for such intervention. Binoy also believed that seminars on disability in air-conditioned city halls would never be able to address the needs of the disabled in rural areas.

Thus was born Urmee's dream, Swabalambi (self-reliant), a community-based organization facilitating services to more than 700 disabled persons in the rural areas of Dimoria block, Kamrup district (metro), which started its work in 1997 with three special educators doing the basic survey with the help of field workers of World Vision, which even provided a space in their office at Sonapur. There were many people with deformities, who were a big burden to their families. Besides describing them as *bemari* (illness), nothing was done to help them cope with life and become productive members of the community. So World Vision spread the word that these *bemari* people and their families could come for counseling held by Swablambi at their office every week. Soon Urmee and her colleagues had their hands full, with people flooding to their center. It was soon evident that none of the disabled were ever taken to a doctor for assessment and therapy. Families were wary of coming to the city for treatment and had no intention of spending their hard-earned money in seeking a cure. Till the parents were alive, the disabled had a roof over their heads and three meals a day. There had been a series of deaths, all of disabled persons, in the area, underscoring how bleak the situation was.

"After we came to know about the fate of the disabled in the villages, I was haunted by the thought that I should have started this work earlier. Without wasting a moment, I began Swablambi's preliminary work, which was to convince the villagers that disability was not a disease and that was why it could not be cured. We started health camps, and doctors of different departments of the Guwahati Medical College and Hospital came as volunteers to clear misconceptions and change mindsets. As the patients were examined, we found that a lot of them required corrective surgery.

A boy with a severe ear infection needed to be operated, and a boy who moved in the kneeling position with the help of a bamboo pole had to have his knees rectified by surgery. We offered help to people with cleft palates, including a patient who had complicated hip surgery. We offered therapy to children with cerebral palsy. We taught them that mentally retarded people needed to pick up self-help skills of cleaning, eating, and grooming."

"But believe me, it was not easy. These simple, unlettered village folk were fearful at the prospect of surgery, of letting their dear ones be 'cut open' as they said, by doctors. What if the illness was still not cured, or if the patient died on the operating table? It took us a while to convince the people that we were not playing with their lives, that the surgeries had a high success rate and would reduce their disabilities. I told them that I myself had gone through seven major surgeries for my polio, that too at a very young age."

After two months, families with patients entered the Guwahati Medical College and Hospital. Urmee and her team were at hand to guide them through the bewildering maze of wards, corridors, and wings, do the necessary paperwork, boost their morale, and attend to the smallest detail. There were people who often got lost in the vast complex and were close to tears.

"From 1997 to 2002, we were busy identifying all categories of disabilities in the 12 *gaon* (village) *panchayat*s of Dimoria Block. There were just a few of us and very little money to go around, but the thought that we could make a difference in their lives motivated us to work hard. After three years of work we got grants from the Ministry of Science and Technology and Ministry of Social Justice and Empowerment, New Delhi. We were now able to recruit local youth as resource persons to train the disabled youth in skills and trades that are viable in the market. We offered special education for children with disabilities, integrated children in primary schools, ensured health care and corrective surgeries. As the years passed, we became like a family, our lives interlinked, as we shared all our joys and sorrows. Now Swabalambi is affectionately named as Bikalanga office and our staff as Bikalanga doctors. There were sponsors for the corrective surgeries, and they met with the families of patients. They include Guwahati Refinery, Oil and Natural Gas Corporation (ONGC), Numaligarh Refinery, and many others. Funding from CARITAS India has upgraded the status of the organization as an established community-based organization utilizing foreign funds to carry on activities involving the *gaon panchayats*, the Development Block, government officials of the block, government teachers, Integrated Child Development Services (ICDS) officials and so on in the rehabilitation program for persons with disabilities and mainstreaming them. We have also collaborated with VAANI, the deaf children's foundation in Kolkata. I have myself been a trainer with VAANI's Brinda Krishna. With their help, we have worked to develop cognitive ability and total communication with families, peers, and the community. Our workers are trained in the Indian Sign Language and vocabulary for the deaf. As a result, many deaf children have broken out of social isolation."

"If there is one goal that I long to achieve, it is that Swabalambi becomes a recognized resource center on all categories of disabilities in Assam in the near future."

***

It is a bright, sunny April morning when we arrive at Swabalambi's main community center at Mohmara Road in Sonapur, near the Forest Range Office. Started in 1977, it encompasses 120 villages in the Dimoria Block and covers 12 *gaon* (village) *panchayats*. It is based on community-based rehabilitation (CBR) where Disable Persons Organizations (DPOs) are deployed to identify the disabled people in their own communities and bring them to Swabalambi to help in their empowerment. Earlier, workers and helpers of Swabalambi used to carry out this process. But now, with the setting up of Community-Based Rehabilitation Program, which is a highly scientific and decentralized method of penetrating interior areas, disabled volunteers work for the improvement of their kind. This has been established as an effective way, especially because it is also very transparent. As the level of awareness has increased, PWDs are demanding their rights and the benefits to which they are entitled.

Urmee and her band of helpers cope with numerous difficulties, big and small, in their day-to-day work. Their Sonapur office suffered extensive damage during two violent storms. In 2005, a fierce gale blew away the roof, which had to be built again.

There are other difficulties that slow down their work. To ensure that all PWDs are provided with the requisite help, DPOs are deployed to identify them. Then they are taken to Mahendra Mohan Chowdhury Hospital at Pan Bazar, Guwahati, where they are examined by a qualified doctor. Then they are issued an identity card that they must produce in order to avail of all benefits given by the government in different schemes.

"But unfortunately," says Urmee, "there are no special funds provided by the government. There is instead, a Disability Pension, which is ₹6,000 per year and is indeed a pittance." The most glaring example of the government's apathy can be understood by the lack of utility services for PWDs in most public places. They are not extended free travel benefits. Children with mental retardation who are below 14 years of age are given a measly ₹500 per month. The same amount of money is payable under the unemployed pension for PWDs above 18 years of age. School-going children with disabilities are given ₹1,500 every six months. We at Swabalambi work hard to provide corrective surgery and have enabled 3,000 cleft-lip operations. We also provide hearing aid, wheel chairs, and tricycles. Pharmaceutical companies and organizations like Shankar Nethralaya undertake programs where cataract operations and other services are offered.

"Our commitment to persons with disabilities is total. After proper counseling we try our best to ensure that they lead normal, productive lives. Once the degree of their disability is assessed, they are trained in various fields so that they are integrated in society and can earn their own livelihood. The family members, teachers, and friends of PWDs are also trained so that they can help them".

At Swabalambi, men usually engage in jute, bamboo craft, screen printing, operating Xerox machines, photography, piggery, candle making and so on, while the womenfolk engage in embroidery, stuffed toy making, cutting and stitching, weaving, fruit preserving, and all local trades. The objects they make are displayed and sold at various expos and fairs.

In many ways, Urmee is the benevolent but exacting matriarch who presides over her family with quiet authority and gentleness. She recently organized a grand wedding for the two lovebirds, Jogesh Rahang and Nilima, who now look after the center at Sonapur. Both suffer from cerebral palsy, but Jogesh excels in making jute products. There are in total 15 salaried employees to help the disabled. Among them is Bipin Das who has palsy in his right hand. He is a CBR worker and a trainer for deaf children. He has been with the center since its formative years and he specializes in bamboo craft.

Then there is Rita Deka, who is a DPO leader. She has locomotor disability on one side but has won laurels in swimming and basketball. At one time she was unable to look after herself, but now she can even help others, thanks to Swabalambi. While Rumi is a coordinator of deaf children, Runu Gogoi is an Indian Sign Language (ISL) trainer.

Swabalambi teems with brave, hardworking people with many inspirational stories. "Take the case of Sunita Nayar," says Urmee, "her parents were so disappointed when she was born that once on a boat trip on the Brahmaputra, her father advised her mother to throw her into the river. But she has overcome most of her locomotor disability to become the vice-president of the DPOs."

That afternoon we attended a meeting attended by PWDs, the newly elected *panchayat* members, and Swabalambi workers. There is animated discussion on *panchayat* schemes for social development,

BPL cards for PWDs, and disability pensions. Several spoke out about the government not providing funds and anomalies suffered by persons with various disabilities. Volunteers moved about serving food with care.

The UNCRPD Act has undertaken the obligation to ensure and promote the full realization of all human rights and fundamental freedom for persons with disabilities without any discrimination. Urmee and her team undertook the task of translating this act into the vernacular language and have organized workshops and raised public awareness of disability rights. In the Census of 2001, it was estimated that the record of disability was just 2 percent and so there was a very meager budget allocated for the disability sector. Urmee got to work, with her enumerators fanning out in all directions to gather the correct estimate. So the accurate figures were included in the 2011 Census, leading to more effective policy and increase in budget allocation.

Helping afflicted villagers to avail of medical aid was a turning point for Swabalambi. Urmee and her team formed a wonderful rapport with the villagers. Till today Swabalambi has been able to identify and treat 700 disabled people. They have also linked up with other agencies that provide artificial limbs, hearing aids, crutches, wheelchairs, tricycles, and other equipment. Arming them with a trade helps them to be self-dependent. So Urmee's training center was born. Children and adolescents with disability are trained for pre-vocational and vocational skills needed to design clothes and make bamboo cane and jute artifacts. They sent raw materials, identify shapes and sizes, choose colors, and learn the concepts of time and money. Urmee is careful to allot tasks according to individual capacity. Only those with moderate-to-mild disability are involved in more intricate cane, bamboo, and jute craft, weaving in handlooms, tailoring, machine embroidering, and so on. Their products have been displayed and sold in various exhibitions, International Trade Fair, and Fabindia. Urmee has also worked hard to create products that are likely to appeal to a discerning clientele, like bread baskets, fruit baskets, and so on. Many of the workers are primary earners of their families.

Every weekend, students, doctors, and well-wishers visit Swabalambi's office at Sonapur. They share a meal with the disabled youth and appreciate their skills. Many among these youth have won medals in the Abilympics (Olympics of Abilities of Persons With Disabilities) held in New Delhi every year.

The little girl who dragged her limp leg behind her as she struggled to keep pace with her playmates is today a source of strength and support to countless others similarly afflicted. Urmee is upbeat about the future, refuses to dwell on her frailties, and dreamily sums it all up. "As I look back on my life, I feel what I have desired the most is to be more than what I am at a certain moment. I have always fought against pettiness and idleness. Every day I seek to expand my boundaries—to feel more, learn more. I am always wanting to grow, improve, expand. And it is this which always fills me with energy and hope. And in spite of everything, I feel truly blessed."

6

How Green Are the Hills?
Bertha G. Dkhar

It is a two-hour journey to Shillong from Guwahati by road, a journey I have undertaken countless times, as a child on my mother's knee, as a daydreaming teen discovering magic in meandering streams, as a mother scolding her boys for poking their elbows out of the car windows. It has always been a journey of hope, of anticipation and renewal. As the highway winds its way up the hill, time past, present, and future coalesce into a single gleaming entity. Range upon range of hills are outlined against a sky awash with a shifting panorama of clouds—ash grey or pearl-tinted. There are tiny tea stalls and in their dark interiors you see gleaming teapots, tumblers, and bottles of biscuits, with a rosy-cheeked, *jensem* (Khasi female attire)-wearing Khasi lass perched in attendance. Hugging the slopes are tin-roofed cottages, poetic in their utter poverty, and on the front are little children in rags, waving at the car, the older ones always carrying the younger siblings tied to a shawl on their backs. Then you pass through small villages and cross stone quarries, cement factories, yellow earth-cutters looking like monster insects, terraced fields on the hill slopes, straggly fences surrendering to wilderness, trucks parked by the roadside, a church, a school, shops selling provisions, firewood, plums, pineapples, strawberries, and jars of bamboo shoot pickled in oil.

Before you know it, the first pine trees appear in view, the temperature drops a little. You are climbing steadily, the sun disappears behind a bank of clouds. There is a sprinkle of raindrops on your windscreen. Then, to your left appears the Umiam Lake, a flat silvery sheet of glass, blue, green, and looking placid, awakening memories of long ago picnics by its banks, of lost friends whom we have not seen for decades, and ghost stories of lovers rising from its secret depths on moonlit nights. The temperature drops even as you cross the dam and shift gears to climb higher. The pines flanking the road are nodding in the breeze. Here and there you spot a forlorn cross in memory of some unfortunate soul borne away by some accident. You lose sight of the lake and then it appears again in a gap between the nodding trees. It's still beauty never fails to move you to the point of tears, pushing you to a yearning for time to stand still, for the unfolding vista of water and hills and trees to be yours forever. Your eyes take in the rolling expanse before you . . . the hills farthest away are blue, almost obscured by fog, then nearer, are the darker green, full of impenetrable forests, and the nearest are an emerald green, sloping down to the white sands, skirting the lake. In no time at all, the car turns a bend on the road, and Shillong is upon you, its twisting streets choked with cars, hunks of fresh beef hanging from hooks in a Mawlai meat shop, uniformed children hopping and skipping along the pavements, taxis crammed with passengers, old landmarks changed, and enormous billboards making promises. In front of a glass-fronted shop with stylish mannequins, a wizened old man in patched trousers and shabby coat roasts corn cobs on a brazier.

There is a special reason why I have taken pains to describe all that I have seen on this journey. There is more, much more to this than what appears to be sentimental scribbling to while away idleness, for this is a journey undertaken to meet a stranger and hear her story, her version of the events that have shaped her destiny and made her what she is. Her name is Bertha Gyndykes Dkhar, a 52-year-old Khasi woman, a pillar of the society and a Padmashri award winner. Bertha has traveled from Shillong to Guwahati much more than I have. But it does not matter to her how the clouds drift among the blue hills or the waters shimmer on the Umiam lake. She does not notice the wild spring cascading down the ancient rocks or the valley spread hundreds of feet below. For Bertha cannot see. Hers is a world of irredeemable darkness, and she has to fashion her reality with sounds, voices, and what her hands can feel. I have to come to hear from her how this tragedy befell her and how she turned around the bleak circumstances of her life into a triumphant saga of service to others. Afflicted by a rare condition called retinitis pigmentosa, a progressive degeneration of the retina, Bertha became totally blind when she was pursuing her postgraduate studies in Bangalore. Forced to relocate to her hometown Shillong, she desperately searched for a teacher's job, but was turned down on the assumption that her condition would prevent her from carrying out her duties. This was the unfortunate case of a young woman who had till recently been pursuing her Master in Social Work and dreaming of rendering service in the field of psychiatry and who suddenly found herself at a dead end. For a time, desperate to earn a living, she even took to selling jams and pickles. She could not help feeling demeaned and worthless.

Then, in 1998, a door opened, and light shone through. Bethany Society, an NGO, appointed her as the headmistress of the Jyoti Sroat School for the visually impaired. From having nothing to do and feeling bitter as dreams crumbled to dust, Bertha moved to a life of responsibility and order. She felt deeply the affliction of her visually disabled charges and experienced the driving need to dispel their darkness with the light of knowledge and enlightenment. But straightaway she ran into a roadblock. There was no Braille in the Khasi script. All students have to pass the mandatory Khasi paper in their board exams. There had to be a way, and soon Bertha had it figured out. In order to help herself, and the children, she would have to learn Braille in English first.

In order to truly appreciate Bertha Dkhar's remarkable work, it is necessary to understand what Braille is. The Wikipedia describes Braille as a writing system used by the blind and the visually impaired that is used for books, menus, signs, elevator buttons, and currency. Users can write Braille with the original slate and stylus or type it in a Braille writer, such as a portable Braille note taker, or on a computer that prints with a Braille embosser.

Braille is named after its creator. Frenchman Louis Braille, who went blind following a childhood accident. At the age of 15, Louis developed his code for the French alphabet in 1824 as an improvement on night writing. He published this system, which subsequently contained musical notations, in 1829. The second revision, published in 1837, was the first digital (binary) form of writing.

Bertha painstakingly learnt English Braille. That was only the first step. Two years later, after intense effort and innovation, she invented the Braille code for the Khasi language. The effort demanded a lot from her, and she soldiered on, drawing on her reserves of patience and limitless capacity for hard work. After the initial shock of descending into a pitch-dark world, she slowly, painfully forced herself to avoid self-pity and look on her tragedy as a challenge and opportunity to see things for herself.

Creating a Braille script in Khasi was a God-send for her visually disabled students. Now able to study the Khasi paper, they began to dream of a better future, one in which they would be empowered to look after themselves and live a life of dignity.

But the struggle was far from over. The Jyoti Sroat School for the visually impaired had 100 blind students and another 50 who were sighted. The school provided free education to its students. There was a perennial shortage of funds, and many good teachers were leaving as they were not getting a decent salary. Even after two decades of its existence, the school has not received any funds from the state government. Bertha is filled with love and concern for her charges. The world was callous and insensitive toward them. But rather than sequestering them from the outside world,

Bertha carried out her mission for inclusive schooling. Her school, therefore, has sighted as well as visually impaired students, and there is a constant effort to sensitize and integrate the two. As she says, "Having separate schools for the blind is not the answer. We need to accommodate them in regular schools to assimilate them in the mainstream. I will continue to fight every day of my life to ensure that one day we have inclusive education."

The angst and desperation of the early years, when her young life was blighted by the curse of darkness, have given way to mellow grace and faith in her destiny. As she said so herself in an interview, "I am proud to be a woman because my Creator believes that the work I am doing can be done best by a female heart and I am proud to work for that belief."

Quietly, in this remote corner of the country, Bertha was scripting an inspirational saga of grace under fire, a living embodiment of adversity turning into a blessing. She caught the attention of the entire nation, when, on March 24, 2012, she was honored with the CNN IBN and Reliance Foundations Real Heroes award. The award celebrates the undying spirit of ordinary people who have rendered extraordinary service and expanded the realm of humanity. The award carried a sum of ₹500,000, which Bertha promptly invested in her school. One of her prized possessions is the letter given to her by the awards committee. It read, "Your exceptional support for the well-being of others in our country has contributed in numerous ways. We take this opportunity to thank you for your selfless contribution in reflecting the spirit of a true Indian." More important, recognition has come from the government, and she was awarded the Padmashri in 2010.

I meet Bertha on a bright, sunny May morning. The road in Shillong is flanked by trees aflame with lavender blossoms. The Shillong correspondent of *The Assam Tribune*, Raju Das, accompanies me to the Jyoti Sroat School. It is like any other school, with a sprawling campus. There are color swings, banana slides, and roundabouts. Uniformed children sit in the classroom drawing, listening, fidgeting in their chairs, nudging each other, whispering, just the way all children do. I am led to Bertha's room by a teacher. The woman who smiles at me is petite, with cropped hair, a round face with fine lines, large, intense eyes, and a hesitant smile. She shakes my hand in greeting, and we sit down to go through her life and the unexpected turns it has taken. Her voice is pleasant and her sentences crisp, understated. When she wants to make a point she leans forward. She often picks up her phone from the table in front of her and clasps it, before putting it down again. She speaks with quiet authority, her dark eyes fixed unseeingly on me.

"My father was the late S.R. Gyndykes, and my mother is Alma G. Gyndykes. I am the eldest of four children. My sisters are Erratha and Flovrette. My mother named my baby brother Homer Richie. Like his namesake, the Greek poet Homer, he too is blind—and writes poetry."

"Strangely enough, my name Bertha means bright. We are Grand Evangelists by faith, and my parents were well-educated people. My mother was a sub-inspector of schools. The four of us were brought up to respect authority, do our duty, and understand the value of discipline in our daily life. Nothing in our household was unplanned. Our mother always laid out healthy, nutritious food on the table—oats, toast, and porridge for breakfast and soups and boiled vegetables for lunch and dinner. My mother was for a time headmistress of the Khasi Janitia Presley Girls School. She taught English and played the piano beautifully. My mom and dad made sure that we stuck to a schedule, with fixed times for meals, study, household work, and play. Once I carelessly threw my school uniform on the floor. My dad made me pick it up 10 times. He was the sectional officer of the Intelligence Bureau and was often away on work. But when he was home he cooked us breakfast and pottered about in the garden."

"As we grew up, we began to resent our parents' strict rules. I, for one, began to rebel and challenged their authority. I hated being dictated to. Even now, I find it hard to say yes easily."

"But then, there was a much more serious problem that consumed me and caused all of us so much heartbreak. At five years of age I was attending St. Joseph School. In the classroom I could hardly make out what the teacher was writing on the blackboard. The faces of my fellow students seemed to be just a blur. At night, my family noticed that I often bumped against the furniture and fall down, hurting myself."

"The eye specialist at Shillong told my parents I was severely short-sighted. Heavy myopia was the word he used. By now I could not see at all with my left eye. My parents, desperate to restore my eyesight, took me to hospitals all over the country every winter. My dad's job at the Intelligence Bureau (IB) helped us to do that. I remember we even went to the famous Sitapur Eye Hospital in Uttar Pradesh, which was set up in 1926. Everywhere they said I had myopia. The power in my glasses kept changing. I felt myself unattractive. I did not have my sister Erratha's beauty, and on top of that, I wore powerful glasses that magnified my eyes. I was also not tall enough to be attractive. I became the butt of jokes. I was named Bottle Specs because my glasses looked like the bottoms of glass bottles. They also called me cow's eyes, because the spectacles, as I have said before, magnified my eyes. I was hurting inside, hurting and raging as shapes, faces, everything slowly began to waver and blur. Unable to blend in with my peers, smarting at the sting of their cruel barbs, I clung to my books, studying diligently. It paid off. I was now on top of my class. I got a double promotion twice and when they wanted to promote me once more, my mother refused, saying that I would be under too much pressure. So there I was, studying with girls two years older than me. My favorite subjects were English and Geography. But I could see only with the greatest difficulty. I began to walk in a zigzag manner, playing the piano became a torture, as I could not follow the notations on the sheet music. Doing sums was also very tough. But I loved to read; Enid Blyton and Ernest Hemingway were my favorites. Like Hemingway's old man battling the whale, I wasn't one to give up easily."

"At that time we did not realize that blindness was waiting for me. I passed my matriculation and enrolled in St. Mary's College with honors in English. But my teachers advised me to take Education instead, as I would have to read extensively in English honors, something that would be too much for my weakening eyesight. At this time of my life, the principal of St. Mary's College, Mother Ann, had a profound impact. She refused to make allowances for me because of my eyesight. I remember going to her, beaming because I had done very well in my Class XII (then known as pre-university) exams. I expected words of praise and a pat on the back. Instead, she told me gently, but firmly, 'You can still do better than this.' Though her response disappointed me at that moment, looking back, I realize how crucial her comment was in pushing myself to excel and not giving into self-pity."

"Let me tell you, however, that life wasn't entirely dark for me. I went through a wild phase—wearing short dresses, reading racy novels, and buying music records. That was also the time the Khasi Students Union started. The idea of youth power excited me. I was elated by the idea of gaining acceptance by belonging to such a body. I remember how Mother Ann closed the college gates to prevent a demonstration in the college camp. I even remember climbing over the gates once."

"Meanwhile, it was time to know more what was wrong about my eyesight. Dr Jennifer Basaiawmoit, who had been a student of my mother's, finally made the correct diagnosis. I had retinitis pigmentosa, which had damaged my retina. We consulted an eye specialist in Kolkata for a second opinion. He made the same diagnosis, saying it was a very rare condition and heredity played a part in it. Imagine how I, a young woman, would have felt when I was told that I could pass on the disease if I married. So there I was, not only faced with growing blindness but also having to make the decision to remain single for the rest of my life."

"But I was in denial. On a visit to Bangalore, I fell in love with the vast, leafy gardens of Lal Bagh and Cubbon's park and begged my parents to let me study there. They gave in and I enrolled for Masters in Social Work, a two-year course. I was able to write my notes, but very often a classmate had to read texts and notes aloud to me. By now I could barely see. I was as if I was running out of time."

"Then I got involved in community development work at Mairang in West Khasi Hills. I had to sit for an exam held by the Social Welfare Department of Meghalaya. I was interviewed by an IAS officer, and I told him about my condition. He gave me a posting in Shillong. But it was far from easy. I faced opposition from all sides. The world was not mine after all. But how I wanted to be a part of this world, if only they would let me!"

"Then the Central Board of Social Work appointed me as a counselor. There was not much paper work involved and that was a blessing, I thought. The chairperson asked me to appear for an interview. I was grilled by a panel of eight people. One of them cruelly asked, 'How can you work if you cannot see?'"

"It was as if I had hit rock bottom. All my years of struggle seemed futile. Nobody wanted to give me a chance to prove myself. I became bitter, pessimistic, and angry. I lashed out against my family and friends, hurting all with my rages. I stopped going out and stopped taking care of my appearance. There was no pleasure in the normal activities of daily life. It was as if I had reached a dead end."

In order to understand Bertha's predication, one has to understand, at least in rudimentary form, the nature of her condition. What then is retinitis pigmentosa? Simply put, it is an inherited degenerative eye disease that causes severe vision impairment or blindness. The progress into blindness may not be uniform. The later the onset, the more rapid is the loss. It is caused by abnormalities of the photoreceptors. Till date there is no known cure, and patients have to cope with deteriorating vision. The mode of inheritance is determined by family history. Though there is no cure, treatments are available in some countries.

Visually unpaired people suffer many trials and tribulations in India. Going by the latest data available, there are 37 million blind people world-wide. Out of that a staggering 15 million are Indians, making the country home to the world's largest number of blind people. Tragically, 75 percent cases of blindness are avoidable. The country needs 40,000 optometrists, whereas there are only 8,000 of them. We need 2.5 lakh donated eyes every year. But the country's 109 eye banks collect just 25,000 eyes, 30 percent of which are not fit to be used.

Continues Bertha, "I did not realize it then, but I was causing my family a lot of suffering. At this period my mother, through prayer and reflection, had a spiritual epiphany. She established a personal relationship with Christ. She even got in touch with faith healers from America to restore my sight. But I felt betrayed by God, by fate. I no longer believed in going to church and saying my prayers. My mother appeared strong, perhaps that strength came from her faith. We often had loud and bitter arguments over my growing distance from my faith."

"I had too much pride to depend on others for my needs. So I sought the job of a substitute teacher when there was a vacancy in a local school in Shillong. But the headmistress doubted if I could be a good teacher. After all, I kept bumping into furniture, doors, and walls. I could not see if my students were paying attention to me. The children laughed at my clumsiness. But it was a time when I was desperate to earn a living. My father by then was a heart patient. I could not bear it that my mother was having to struggle all alone to support our family."

"It was then that I went to the US. On my return, a ray of light entered my embittered heart. I realized I could not struggle alone anymore. Faith in God would give me the strength to go on." Bertha found solace in Jesus Calls, a ministry dedicated to prayer for the suffering, irrespective of caste, creed, and religion.

It was started by late Brother D.G.S. Dhinakaran to serve the people through the love and compassion of Jesus Christ. Brother D.G.S. Dhinakaran (founder) and M. Paul Dhinakaran (co-founder and president) have made Jesus Calls a worldwide spiritual movement. Dr Paul Dhinakaran has established 37 prayer lovers in India and 11 others throughout the world, where prayers are offered for people in distress. Today millions are blessed through prayers and receive comforting messages of the Dhinakaran through their public meetings, TV programs, Letter Ministry, and personal prayers."

Today, Bertha looks back for her long and turbulent life and finds meaning and purpose in it. She describes to me her daily routine. "My day starts early and I wake up at 4:30 a.m. and have my meditation and prayers till 6:00 a.m. Sometimes I do light exercises and then have my breakfast. Then I start off from home early in the morning at 7:30 a.m. when the school bus picks me up and I am at my school office at 8:30 a.m."

"In the office the routine is not fixed, but there is the usual work."

"I return home at around 5:30 a.m. This is the time I relax at home, but at times I also help with the cooking. I love to bake cakes, make pizzas and cookies. I can make Chinese Indian and continental food. Though I rarely listen to music these days, I enjoy singing a lot. On Sundays I go to church at the Full Gospel Fellowship in Nongrim hills, and there we sing and dance to our hearts' content. I play the piano and it truly relaxes me. I believe and am guided by the Biblical principles on the role of nun and women and that is a man is the head of the family and a woman binds the family together."

"Have I found peace in my life? Yes, I have. When I lost my eyesight things became very difficult, and I slowly learnt to accept my fate after many storms. It was a long and slow process, but today I am at peace. I turned to spiritualism and that gave me the answers to questions that haunted me. I have learnt to be positive in whatever I do."

"I have many wonderful memories in my life. In 1999 I was made headmistress of the Jyoti Sroat School without appearing for an interview! This event and the responsibility it brought with it totally turned my life around. I was chosen in spite of my disability, and I became determined to prove myself. Every day I gave myself 100 percent to this faith reposed on me. I would also like to write a book."

"In the end, blindness does not limit the imagination. I read in Braille the books of Jane Austen and am transported to the beautiful English countryside. The mind is always free and can win over all troubles and sufferings."

7

Mapping the Truth:
Teresa Rehman

Dusk falls gently and the lights bathe the interiors of the university campus quarters with a golden glow. Inside one such house, a young woman quietly goes about preparing supper. Her hair is swept back with a scrunch, and she stirs the bubbling gravy over the gas stove, absently wondering whether her husband would be late returning from work.

Little Tamara is sprawled on the carpet in front of the TV, whooping with glee at the antics of Scooby Doo, while baby Kyra is sleeping snugly in her cot. It is a cozy, domestic scene, with the comforting minutiae of everyday life. And yet, the young wife and mother knows what a fragile thing this peace is, and how, even as she winds down her household for the night, somewhere there are guns blazing, grenades tearing open human bodies, and homes built with love and toil going up in flames.

This young woman has had experiences that most can only imagine, reporting fearlessly from one of the most troubled hotspots of the world—Northeast India.

Life for Teresa Rehman often seems to be lifted straight from the pages of a thriller. She remembers traveling deep into Hebron in interior Nagaland, escorted by a man with an AK 47 to meet Th Muivah, chief of the National Socialist Council of Nagaland,

Issak Muivah. All along the way she pestered the man with questions, which he deftly sidestepped. Her one to one with Muivah was a resounding success. She was able to probe deeply into his ideology, his strategy, and his hopes for the future of Nagaland. He was amazed to find that this intense and fearless young woman knew all about his love for pork and his gradual conversion to vegetarianism.

If one day she is caught in the crossfire between the Indian Army and the Nationalist Socialist Council of Nagaland—Isak-Muivah (NSCN-IM) faction in Nagaland, the next day she is unearthing why so many tea-garden laborers are dying of tuberculosis. As she listens to a disconsolate Manipuri woman describe how her school-going son was kidnapped by militants to work as a child soldier, an armed officer bursts into the hut, demanding to see her ID. Faced with a barrage of questions, a much-feared insurgent leader mutters to his aide, "This reporter is very cunning."

This backhanded compliment aside, Teresa Rehman's work as a journalist has been widely acknowledged. She was honored with the Ramnath Goenka Excellence in Journalism Award 2008–2009 for the category, "Reporting on the JK and the Northeast (print)," the Sanskriti Award 2009 for Excellence in Journalism, and the Seventh Sarojini Naidu Prize for Best Reporting on Panchayati Raj by the Hunger Project. Also awarded the Wash, Kunjabala Devi, and Laadli awards, she has widely traveled and has worked with leading media houses of India like *India Today*, the *Telegraph*, and *Tehelka*.

On a lazy summer afternoon, surrounded by books, cushions, magazines, her laptop, and packets of takeaway Chinese, Teresa leads me to where it all began. "My early years were spent in the lap of pristine nature in a quaint place—Sumer in Meghalaya." She begins, "I remember my mother encouraging us to read a lot of books. I used to eagerly wait for my maternal aunt, as she used to get an assortment of story books for us. I used to live a dual life—that of an ordinary school-going child and that of imaginary characters of Enid Blyton books. I feel all this helped me to explore the unbidden and come up with something fresh and delightful." Journalism, with all its challenges, seemed right up her street.

"I don't know why, but I was always fascinated by journalists and journalism. There was no journalist in the family who could inspire me. But I used to rummage through my mother's collection of magazines, *Illustrated Weekly of India*, *Reader's Digest*, and *India Today*, and used to imagine myself in one of the bylines. I started writing regularly in the children's supplements of the local newspapers and turned into a child celebrity. There was no stopping me after that. There was a dogged determination to become a journalist, which never impressed my dad. The line-up of accolades and awards could finally convince my father to forgive me for not becoming a doctor!"

"Though I started out as a cub reporter in the local dailies of Assam, where I was writing in the children's supplements, my innings as a full-fledged journalist started with the *India Today* magazine in 2000, where I joined as a trainee journalist. Though I was on the desk, I tried ways and means to do stories, as reporting was my first love. After one-and-a-half years, I came back to Assam due to certain compelling domestic circumstances. I started working as a correspondent for *The Telegraph*, where I handled the Feature page. I did all kinds of reporting here, right from covering a local football match to an investigative story on the State Home for Women. I decided to take a break for four years when I had my first child. Then I joined *Tehelka* news magazine as its Northeast India Correspondent, where I worked for four years and managed to do some path-breaking stories. I did hardcore conflict reporting, apart from the regular stuff on culture, politics, society, and the environment. This fetched me several accolades."

"Then I decided to do some independent work. I started doing media analysis for www.thehoot.org, writing for the *Women's Feature Service* and a series on climate change for *Reuters*. Somehow, I feel the region does not get its due space in the so-called national dailies." She decided to create her own space. She then turned a media entrepreneur with her own baby, an online news magazine www.thethumbprintmag.com. "It is a dream I am trying to live in its different hues. We called ourselves an international magazine with a northeastern soul. We are a start-up venture and still struggling to stay afloat. We hope to grow not just in numbers and figures but as an institution which will leave its thumbprints in the sands of time."

She vehemently denies that women make better journalists. "There can be only good journalists and bad journalists, gender does not matter. But yes, women are generally more sensitive and empathize better with victims, be it in a conflict situation or a disaster. However, it is still a male-dominated profession and most policy decisions are taken by males." She also feels that women do have problems that are specific to their gender, like lack of separate toilets in the workplace, maternity leave, and a crèche for their children, which compel many of them to leave their career mid-way.

"One mantra to be a good journalist is humility. We should be ready to travel in an overcrowded bus or have food by a road-side eatery or even sleep in a haystack. We will have to shed our prejudices in order to report objectively." Teresa seeks inspiration from unusual quarters. "Somehow, the famous and visible journalists don't impress me. I find women scribes working in grueling situations, especially those trying to carve out a niche for themselves more appealing. For instance, I had met a Pakistani journalist who happened to be the first journalist writing on environmental issues in the Urdu press. She wanted to take these vital issues to the masses. She thus broke new ground and withstood the cynicism of her editors who were doubtful readers wanted to read such news."

"Women journalists also seem to be more resilient when working in adverse circumstances. A group of Afghan women scribes, when asked about their difficulties, one of them said, 'We have to make the best of what we have.' An elderly woman from

Bangladesh told me how she had been ostracized because she was a journalist."

"Figuring out which stories need to be explored and reported is of crucial importance. The underlying thought is that it must be something not reported about that place in any newspaper previously and is unknown to the rest of the country and the world. Added to this is that there is a huge accountability that the story must be in the larger interest of the society. I try to look at the nooks and corners that others don't care about. We must keep our ears, eyes, nose, and most of all, our eyes open."

"To get a good story, one need not travel far. There are good stories lying in our backyard. For instance, my story, which got me the WASH Media Award 2010, given by the Geneva-based Water Supply and Sanitation Collaborative Council (WSSCC) and the Stockholm International Water Institute, was based on the horrors my domestic help had to face when she has to do something as basic as answering the call of nature during floods. I got a story that appealed to a global audience right at my home."

There is some measure of stereotypical presentation of the Northeast in the mainstream media. I ask her whether she has tried to counter this.

"I am not sure I have succeeded. Other journalists are making an effort too. Giving the real picture of the Northeast is a collective responsibility of all journalists not only in the region but the rest of the country and world too."

"Though conflict is an important part of reporting from the region, but it is not the only thing happening. There are so many human interest stories waiting to be told, stories of the common people and their struggles, which are callously marginalized by the mainstream media. Reversing stereotypes cannot happen overnight. It calls for consistent efforts by all journalists; we must be able to package the stories in exciting ways."

One of the highlights of Teresa's remarkable journalistic career was winning the Seventh Sarojini Naidu Prize for best reporting on women in Panchayati Raj on October 2, 2007. This prestigious award has been instituted by the Hunger Project, and Teresa at that time was principal correspondent (Northeast India). The prize honors the commitment and contribution of the media in show-casing the work of these elected women. The Hunger Project has trained thousands of elected women to enable effective leadership in bringing water, basic health, hygiene, and education to their villages. Teresa's story focused on Hema Kumari Das, a *panchayat* president from Rajabari village in Assam, who had strived for the upliftment of primary education in a village inhabited by the Mishing community, who were internally displaced people. This story reaffirms Teresa's belief that the best stories are waiting to be explored in the most obscure places. In her skilled hands, these testimonies acquire a universal resonance.

She now opens up about the emotional trauma when reporting from conflict zones.

"My story on a fake encounter in Imphal, the capital of Manipur, was such an instance. This is a story that changed my life. The story jolted me to the realities of reporting on a conflict zone—the total lack of a support system, both legal and physical. There is a fear factor that is very real and palpable. There seems to be no redressal of the conflict that journalists face in their line of duty."

On the upside, didn't journalism give her the scope to travel across the world?

"Certainly, I have traveled to almost all the continents. I have many fond memories of crossing the border between India and Pakistan on foot. I remember the delicious roadside tea in Istanbul, Turkey. The warmth and hospitality of the common people rebuts the hostility created by the media and politicians. I was pained by the slums, the filth, and squalor in Nairobi, Kenya. Watching homeless people in America was very unsettling. School dropouts in Baltimore were engaged in deadly gun fights. It was also inter-esting to see black women shaving off their woolly hair in summer to save the trouble of managing them."

Now it is time to talk about her new baby, thumprintmag.com. "Listen to the color of your dreams," strummed the Beatles in their album *Tomorrow Never Knows It*. "It seems incredible that I am living a dream in its different shades and hues. Sitting at my home in a district in Assam, a state in India's Northeast, this online news magazine on a shoestring budget is making its presence felt in cyberspace and winning the hearts of people around the world. Such is the power of the Internet. We want to tell the world that the Northeast is not a museum. We are not another killing field. We are a vibrant and living world with moments of joy and sorrow. We are men, women, and children who wish to tell our own stories and take them to the world and bring the world closer to us. We plan to go global with local stories, tales of the marginalized, the underreported, crisscrossing through geographical terrain and psychological barriers." She hums the famous John Lennon number. "You may say I am a dreamer, but I'm not the only one. I hope someday you'll join us. And the world will be as one."

She acknowledges the supportive role of her family. "I am a mother of two daughters. My husband, an academic, is very supportive. He takes care of the kids when I am not around. I am a roving reporter, mother, and wife. My parents have always encouraged me in my pursuits in life."

She then talks about the story that changed her life forever, involving a fake encounter in Manipur. "I titled the story as 'Murder in Plain sight,' and it had a series of tell-tale photographs showing a minute-by-minute account of how an unarmed young man was accosted by policemen and shot dead in a pharmacy in a busy marketplace. Later the police gave an official version that the young man was responsible for a shoot-out in the same location and, hence, was killed in an encounter. Usually such official versions are difficult to disprove, though everyone may know them to be false, but in an almost unprecedented coincidence, a local photographer was present at the scene and managed to shoot a minute-by-minute account of the alleged encounter."

"The photographs reveal that the young man was actually calmly standing as the commandoes frisked him, took him to the pharmacy, and later brought out his dead body. The photographer was petrified and did not want to reveal his identity, though he wanted the news to be published, and no media outlet in Manipur would publish it. So he approached me, as I was in the adjacent state of Assam and represented a national media house. These 12 photographs, exposing a shocking truth, was what journalists dream of. It was the biggest scoop imaginable and was picked up by the global media worldwide. In Manipur, the story highlighted the years of repression the common people have suffered and there was a mass civil uprising. But personally, I was at a low ebb. The grisly photographs haunted me, and I could not sleep for days. I started getting feelers that there was an imminent threat to my life too. I felt very vulnerable. I got to know that the state was gunning for the anonymous photographer. I was very concerned for his safety. I even got a copy of the Indian Penal Code and the Criminal Procedure Code to think of ways and means to protect myself and the photographer."

"After the uprising, came the reprisal. I had to face a threat, daring me to go to Manipur again. The threat came from authorities in the state (I do not wish to make their names public); I still remember how I met the officials of the Special Investigative Team from Manipur in the local police station in Guwahati, my hometown (I thought it would be the safest place for me and I did not have an office). As I refused to go to Manipur after the threats to face the one-man judicial commission inquiring into the case, the commission, in an unprecedented move, held a special sitting for me in Guwahati. The Central Bureau of Investigation (CBI) also questioned me in Guwahati as I refused to go to Imphal. Physically too I was not keeping well, as I was pregnant. My reluctance to go to Manipur in such a condition was also due to the fact that the state is under the Armed Forces (Special Powers) Act 1950 (AFSPA), giving them the power to interrogate and harass me with impunity."

"In a positive sign, 14 months after Chungkham Sangit Singh Meitei was killed in a fake encounter by the Manipur police, the CBI filed a chargesheet against nine of the 14 accused policemen. The magazine *Tehelka* also won the prestigious IPI-India Award for Excellence in Journalism 2010 for this very story."

"Covering conflict from an underreported region like the Northeast of India can spring surprises at every step. As a journalist trying to look beyond the surface, I have often written off dreary government press releases that scrolls down mere statistics of the number of militants killed and arms and ammunition recovered. Instead, I have tried to delve into the inner psyche of the real people—the human faces who are either part of or are victims of violence inflicted by state or non-state actors."

"My work has constantly exposed me to danger. It is also a very lonely battle, running for legal advice and also a psychologist to deal with the emotional trauma. There is no support system for journalists in ground zero."

"There are stories that haunt you long after they have receded to the past. I met a mother in Thoubal district of Manipur, who told me how her boy did not return home from school. The insurgents had kidnapped him to make him one of their child soldiers. The outfit later claimed that the boys joined of their own accord. In states like Manipur, more than 20 militant outfits operate, and editors have been gunned down and newspaper offices closed. Mediapersons have to face the ire of both the state and the militants."

"Reporting hardcore conflict also entails visiting militant camps, which, of course, has its own share of adventure. Meeting the female cadres is an intriguing experience, but most of them are lower-rank cadres waiting to serve tea and cook lunch. For the militants it is an equally intriguing experience to talk to a journalist, that too a woman. Once I was returning from a designated camp of a militant outfit in ceasefire in Assam. A member of the publicity wing called me and asked me to stop wherever I was. I stopped the car at a small marketplace and waited for them to turn up.

I was very apprehensive of what was to follow. Then a car came and the occupants beckoned me. I was stunned when they thrust an envelope into my hands. The man looked very uncomfortable and told me not to open the envelope as it contained important papers. On my journey back I opened the envelope and found a wad of currency notes! They had actually tried to bribe me into writing good things about them! I somehow managed to send back the envelope."

"Sadly, the media projects the Northeast as one homogenous, trouble-torn frontier. It does not bother to look closely into why young Indian citizens are taking up arms against the state. They do not ask why Ima Gyaneswari and 11 other women protested against the AFSPA by stripping in front of the Assam Rifles headquarters. I have had my share of meeting top militant leaders. I met Th Muivah, chief of the NSCN-IM at the council headquarters in Hebron, some 40 km from Dimapur. I bombarded him with questions like what kind of person he was, his love of pork, his gradual conversion to vegetarianism, and whether his religious beliefs clashed with his cause. I also asked the lower cadres to play the keyboard and drums for me. Their discipline and devotion to the cause was clearly apparent."

During the course of her work, Teresa also busts some myths that give the false impression that women in the Northeast are liberated and empowered, unlike those elsewhere in the country. "There are many communities where women are treated as mere commodities. Most of the tribes of Northeast India adhere to age-old customary laws instead of the statutory laws in matters of matrimony, inheritance, and divorce. The unwritten tribal laws are usually recognized as binding by their communities. 'A rotten fence and one old wife can be changed anytime,' goes a Mizo saying. Mizo customary law in regard to divorce is highly anti-women. A divorced women has to leave home penniless, even though she has contributed to the household economy. Among some Arunachal tribes, not only is child marriage practiced but the girl child is considered as a tradable commodity as well, negotiable for a price decided by parents, paid by the man she is married to. Women are not allowed any say in the village decision-making bodies, thus robbing them of both space and justice."

In regard to her identity, that of belonging to a minority community, Teresa says, "Among many Muslim women, I had the privilege of completing my education and pursuing my career. I do not embody any of the stereotypes of a Muslim woman that is generally portrayed in the media. The representation of Muslim women in media continues to be a source of debate."

"In spite of being educated and empowered, I feel my space as a Muslim woman is limited. I feel a pertinent problem faced by Muslim women is the lack of public space as part of the community. I have my space as a journalist, as an activist, as a mother, or as any other woman in society, but I don't have space as another Muslim woman. I was part of a landmark event when the present Governor of Assam J.B. Patnaik led a group of Muslim women to pray inside a mosque at a dargah in Sivasagar, Assam. The event evoked mixed reactions, mostly criticism, without any sound argument. This step led by the Governor of Assam had at least sparked off a debate across a cross-section of society. There is a vacuum in the public and intellectual space for Muslim women. It is not just the act of *namaz* itself, but the space will open many other doors for Muslim women."

"I don't think the community can progress if its individuals are not respected and given equal space. In an already disadvantaged community, women are doubly disadvantaged. We need to address these inherent problems within the community first, as they are directly or indirectly related to the various social, economic, and political problems faced by the community. Women should be encouraged to participate in debates and discussions concerning various issues."

Teresa has clear views on media activism. According to her, social media has definitely changed the way media activism works in a country like India. However, she points out, "The problem arises when the basic distinction between media activism and trial by media is blurred. The Jessica Lal case is a wonderful case of media criticism. If a prosecution gets bogged down for an inordinately long period, the media is certainly entitled, nay, obliged, to probe and expose the causes for the delay. However, determination of the guilt or innocence of a person under our constitutional scheme is the function of the courts, which should not be inspired by the media. During the Arab Spring revolts, a spontaneous yet coordinated activist use of social media developed. Activists established strategic communication spaces through Facebook groups and Twitter hash tags. This is a transmedia world—information knows no boundaries. However, just because the civil rights protests occurred without Twitter, Facebook, and mobile phones doesn't mean a powerful movement for change won't happen with them helping bring people and resources together." She is deeply concerned by the cross commercialization that has engulfed the entire realm of the media. Media is now seen as peddling products rather than conveying ideas and promoting events rather than discussing issues. TRP ratings dictate satellite television. But she feels good work is being done in the online media, which knows no geographical or psychological barriers and can be run on a shoe-string budget.

With the increasing financial presence in India, there are many conglomerations of women, journalists in the country, notably the Network of Women in Media (NWMI) and South Asian Women in Media (SAWM). Teresa is the Joint Secretary of the Indian chapter of the SAWM. As she says, "In examining gender patterns in South Asia, we need to analyze the participation and position of women in the media, and the impact of these positions on women's development. This means women's right to participate in public debates and to have their views heard and the right to be portrayed in the media in ways that accurately represent the complexities of their lives. The convergence of new media technologies and influx of private media organizations in the past decades have increased the number of women working in both print and electronic media. However, women have not gained parity with men in terms of participation and decision-making. Women journalists can become catalysts, defenders, and guardians of women's rights all over."

I am curious to know how political Teresa is. "Man is a political animal," she replies. "Politics pervades all aspects of our lives. I do believe that we need good and efficient people in politics and I see some hope in the young lot. Though I am not neck deep into politics, I do drop in as and when some issue interests me. I find politics a very interesting subject. And I feel students of political science will make good journalists, as they will understand the issues of the state better."

Compared to the angst of her earlier years as a journalist, she feels that she has calmed down somewhat. "I guess its wisdom that comes with age and experience. I do get agitated over injustice and the corruption that has crept into the Indian mind. I am appalled when I see the total lack of scruples in relationships among human beings. I feel we do need to respect some values and age-old wisdom. I guess these are the signs of changing times." In her career, Teresa has consciously tried to do women-related stories. She has tried to give voice to women's silence. Some of her best stories had in fact been created when she pursued it from a woman's point of view. As for being a feminist, she explains, "I am more of a humanist and believe every human being should be treated with dignity. I believe women have rights and should be respected. But I am not a dogmatic feminist who will rebel against everything, who would refuse to look after her husband or look after her children. But yes, if I am denied my rights, I will rebel."

So how is Teresa, the woman inside? "Oh, she is very soft and vulnerable," she confesses. "She loves to be pampered. Hates being alone. Loves it when somebody cooks for her and even serves it for her. She loves being showered with gifts. She enjoys being in social gatherings though she feels quite out of place at times. She enjoys observing others. Can never say no to eating out. Is a shopaholic when she knows there's enough money in the bank; otherwise she can comfortably lead a frugal life. Loves her independence and mental space, which she will never compromise with."

Today Teresa is busy nurturing her two daughters as well as her recent baby, thumprintmag.com. She fills it with stories that make us think of this region in a different way. There is variety, an upsurge of hope, and a realism about the multilayered existence of the people. As Henry Anatole Grunwald put it, "Journalism can never be silent. That is its greatest virtue. It must speak, and speak immediately, while the echoes of wonder, the claims of triumph, and the signs of horror are still there."

She remembers with nostalgia the many unknown and ordinary people whose stories she has given voice to. "I still remember the postman in the river island of Majuli who kept an extra pair of tattered clothes that he used to wade through the muddy flood waters. I will always admire his spirit. And the beautiful Apatani woman with her big nose plugs in Itanagar. It was like opening the pages of a book on anthropology."

"And then there was the old mask-maker in Majuli who gave me intricate details on how to make a mask and his lamenting the fact that mask-making is a dying art. I truly feel the Northeast is a paradise for journalists. There is joy in discovering the untold stories of the common people in every corner of the region."

Looking back on her years of reporting from this region, she says that she was so enthused by her assignments that she never felt tired, either physically or mentally. "There is the joy of writing a report and getting something novel and exciting for my readers. All the travails seem trivial and part of the game. If you want to get the whole story, you have to walk the extra mile, be it driving through bumpy roads or wadding through muddy streams, walking a rickety bridge or getting caught up in a thunderstorm, and even getting in the middle of crossfire between militant groups—as had happened to me."

Not surprisingly, Teresa believes that journalists are born, not made. "Going to a media school and getting trained by some of the best hands in the industry won't make you a great journalist. I do think you need to have real passion for the profession, so much so that you are ready to die for it. But I have to say I am a trained journalist, considering I went to a media school, but I unlearnt many of the theories and broke many rules in the profession."

Although she admits feeling guilty at times for neglecting her daughters, her husband, an environmental scientist, is a hands-on father and loves nothing better than to look after his girls. The hyperactive Teresa finds it hard to switch off. She is either following a new story, watching old movies on television, meditating, doing yoga, or playing with her daughters. As for her coping strategy, she tries to make the best of what she has, dealing with situations as they arise. And she tries to be bold when in a spot. "That," she laughs, "has always worked."

8

Pulling No Punches: Mary Kom

I f you wish to probe into the psyche of the remarkable woman featured here and understand what it took for her to emerge from obscurity to become an international icon, we must begin with a story in the Bible. It is a story she remembers every time she stands face to face with each daunting challenge. The story of David and Goliath inspires and motivates her to use her petite body like a lethal human cannonball. "Like David, I too am small," Mary Kom has earnestly explained in many televised interviews. "And like him, I too am not afraid to fight those that are bigger than me."

"The strength of a woman is not measured by the impact that all her hardships in life have had on her, but the strength of a woman is understood by the extent of her refusal to allow those hardships to dictate to her and who she becomes." These words seem to have been penned with the indomitable Mangte Chungneijang Mary Kom in mind. Born on March 1, 1983, in a remote village of Kangethei in Churachandpur district of the Northeastern state of Manipur, she is the eldest child of a poor tribal family. Her parents, father Mangte Torpa Kom, a former wrestler, and Mangte Akham Kom, her mother, were shifting cultivators who toiled doggedly in their *jhum* (shifting of cultivation) fields, barely managing to provide sustenance for their family of four children. One of Mary's middle names, given by her grandmother, was Chungneijang, which means prosperous. It was a word Mary was intensely aware of from a very young age, and she quietly resolved to do what was required to lift her family from the quagmire of poverty and hardship. As the eldest child, Mary understood her responsibilities very early. A tough, wiry child, she did not think twice about pulling the plough through the muddy fields or lifting bundles of wood to sell in a nearby market. She would sit at the loom and weave *punshi* shawls and *punvei* wraparounds. She caught fish, cooked over smoky wood fires, and even made charcoal to sell to villagers. She was always running from one errand to the other, restless and eager to have some time to play. Her friends often teased that she would give P.T. Usha a tough time. As a student of Loktak Christian Model High School in Moirang, she was indifferent to academics but avidly took part in hockey, football, and athletic events. She was a great fan of martial arts films, and when she saw Muhammad Ali boxing, she had her first epiphany. This was it. Boxing was what she was destined to do. And when fellow Manipuri Dinko Singh won the gold medal in the 1998 Asian Games, it was like a sign from above for this devoutly Christian girl. By then, she had moved to Imphal to train for athletics. Boxing was a sport she took up secretly. At that time, boxing was considered an unladylike sport, and father Mangte Tonpa feared that if she injured her face and marred her looks, no suitor would come forward to marry her. So Mary took the most crucial decision of her life without her father's permission.

At Imphal, she wasted no time in presenting herself at the Sports Authority of India Complex, before the boxing coach, K. Kosama Meitei. Dressed in a torn T-shirt, without proper shoes on her feet, the slender girl plainly looked as if she were in the wrong place. In fact, so unimpressive was she that Kosama refused to let her even speak and waved her away, saying rehearsals were in progress. On the ring, men were sparring, pulling punches, and jabbing in the air. The air crackled with tension. The men's singlets were drenched in sweat. Some had bruises on their faces and arms. Kosama stood watching intently, shouting out encouragement, pulling up someone, and timing the bouts. Hours passed by and when the trainees packed up and left, Kosama was astonished to see the girl still standing close by, her dark eyes meeting his in mute ppeal. After three days, the tough coach melted, but not before varning her that she was about to embark on a dangerous sport; that she would have to fight against men, there being no women trainees; and that she would always have as her opponents boxers who were taller and heavier than her. Mary listened and nodded. Of course, it was so simple. She would just have to be David.

But epiphanies are one thing and reality another. Muhammad Ali's punches looked effortless on television, and here, as her training started, her body was stretched to the limit during the grueling practice sessions. Every muscle cried out for relief, and every bone in her body ached. But the exhilaration of doing what she loved made it all worthwhile. Coach Kosama, moved by the feisty girl, explained all about the sport to her. Boxing was a martial art and combat sport in which two people fought each other, using strength, speed, reflexes, endurance, and will, and throwing punches at each other with gloved hands.

So there was Mary, learning, absorbing the techniques and rules with undivided attention. Returning to her uncle's home, she would lie awake after dinner, reminding herself of the rules. "I must not hit below the belt; I must not hold, trip, push, bite, or spit. I am not allowed to kick, head-butt, and must only hit with the knuckles of a closed fist." Half-way through her memorizing, Mary would drift off to sleep, dog-tired after day's exertions.

Learning what technique suited her was equally challenging. Her coach M. Narjit Singh helped her grasp the basics. "See, girl, no two fighter styles are the same. It all depends on what kind of a body and mind one has. There is the boxer out-fighter. He always puts himself at some distance from his opponent, using jabs and long range punches. Muhammad Ali and Sugar Ray Leonard, they were of this type."

"Then you have the boxer who are punchers. He is a well-rounded boxer who can fight from close range and using several techniques. There are the counter-punchers who are quick to use the mistakes of their opponent to score. The brawlers or sluggers are not very polished but try to win by sheer strength. Infighters stay close to their rivals and use hooks and upper cuts to defeat them. As you learn, you will understand what style works for you."

So Mary immersed herself in the world of the jab and the cross, the hook, and the uppercut. She learnt to slip, sway, duck, lob, and weave and to parry and block. Long after the male trainees left, Mary would be on her feet, dancing up and down, swinging punches at an imaginary foe.

This wiry girl, now in her late teens, was unstoppable. In 2000, she burst into the boxing scene with the Manipur State Boxing Championship. Her father Mangte Tonpa had heard that there was a promising woman boxer belonging to the Kom community. But he had not put two and two together, simply because he could not believe his first born would defy him. Imagine his consternation when her face was splashed in the newspapers after her victory. Cut to the quick, Mangte Tonpa fumed and refused to talk to his daughter. But Mary was not one to give in easily. She had found her calling. Boxing was what she was born to do. Hearing the steely resolve in her voice, he softened and said, "If you believe that, child, then let it be as you say. Your mother and I will try to give whatever you need. Your path is difficult, but you have our blessings." A great weight rolled off Mary's mind that day. She would no longer have to feel guilty and be secretive. She could now concentrate on following her idol Muhammad Ali. And soon she was streaking like a comet, reaching the international level in boxing at 18, just a year after starting formal training. It was an incredible feat. It was also the time to travel light, and she simply called herself Mary, taking much comfort in that it revealed her faith, which was always a key factor in her life.

Before following Mary's meteor-like trajectory, it would be a useful exercise to trace the history of women's boxing. Boxing has always been a male sport, participated in by men, who were not only trained by men but also booed or cheered by an exclusively male audience. The early beginnings of women's boxing are pretty much unchronicled because there was stiff opposition and women did not get to box professionally. The first recorded evidence of women's boxing can be traced to London in the 1720s. But until the 1950s, only sporadic bouts were fought. Moreover, the contestants did not have to adhere to specific rules, and hence, these events were not standardized. In US, the first bout between women boxers was said to have taken place in 1876. In 1904, during the Olympics in St. Louis, US, female boxing was merely an exhibition sport, and only in 2012 did it get recognition as a competitive sport. It must be mentioned that the 1950s witnessed professional female boxing and televised fights became the rage. But it was only as late as in 1993 that US boxing was compelled to recognize and support female boxing and female amateur boxing. Some of the promising female boxers were the legendary Ann Wolfe, Christy Martin, and Laila Ali, daughter of Muhammad Ali.

Today boxing is one of the most popular sports for women. However, women's boxing does not invite wide media coverage. The sport has suffered from marginalization. Unlike men's boxing, the female counterpart lags behind in solid infrastructure, financial backing, and public support.

Obviously there are bound to be some differences in the rules governing male and female boxing. The equipment they use are different and women have some pre-match rules that men do not. Female boxers have to wear both a groin protector and a breast protector while a groin protector suffices for men. Both, however, have to wear a mouthpiece. Female boxers are not allowed to wear make-up during a fight. They are to tie back their hair with soft and nonabrasive materials. They must also undertake a mandatory test to prove they are not pregnant. While male boxing matches range from 4 to 12 rounds, female boxing matches have a maximum of 10 rounds.

In a remote corner of the world, Mary Kom rises to meet her destiny. Her impoverished family cuts corners to ensure a good diet, equipment, and training. The family cow is sold off to pay for her training. After her win in the Manipur State Women's boxing championship in 2000, she swiftly clinches the regional champion title in West Bengal. Since then, the sky has been the limit for Mary, a gawky 18-year-old with her trademark fringe of hair and a face revealing the reserves of strength within, Mary was on the threshold of international fame. She would be flying to cities around the world, places she had never even heard off, meet people of many races, and hear varied tongues. She would taste strange food and handle a bewildering range of currency. There would be flashbulbs popping around her, requests for autographs, thunderous applause, medals around her neck, and trophies in her hands.

Her international debut was at the first AIBA Women's World Boxing Championship in US, where she won a silver medal in the 48-kg-weight category. She was on a winning spree after that, including winning the AIBA Women's World Boxing Championship in Turkey in 2002. In 2004, she won gold at the Women's World Cup in Norway and, in 2005 again, won gold at the Asian Women's Boxing Championship in Taiwan and the AIBA Women's World Boxing Championship in Russia. The following year saw her winning gold at the Venus Women's Boxing Cup in Denmark and the AIBA Women's World Boxing Championship in India. But a bout of illness forced her to stay away from the final of the World Championship, though she was leading 19–4.

But life was not just about jabs and punches, workouts, and sparring. Unknown to Mary, love was waiting to claim her. The man was Onkholer Kom, better known as Onler. He was a student in

Delhi, a leader of the Kom community there, comprising mainly of students and young professionals.

After his graduation from Sankardev College, Shillong, in 2000, Onler worked in the Customs and Central Excise for sometime in the mid-1990s. Later he went to Delhi to study law. At one time he ran an NGO named Rural Development and Relief Centre in his native village Shamu Lamlan in Churachandpur district of Manipur. He has represented football teams of the region under different capacities. In 1999, he lost his mother and resolved to return to Manipur to look after his ailing and elderly father. However, his father expressly told him to continue his studies. At about that time, he also broke up with his girlfriend. In 2001, Onler and Mary's paths crossed, and a beautiful romance blossomed. In the years to come he would be the wind beneath her wings, the rock-steady anchor that provided her the security and assurance she so needed. A silent, soft-spoken man who could display unexpected flashes of humor, Onler was nine-years older than her. In 2001 Mary happened to be in Delhi. She was on her way to participate in the National Games in Punjab. Members of the Kom community met up for an informal interaction. Onler was a student of law at Delhi University. He chatted briefly with Mary. Their association continued. She visited him every time she was in Delhi. He gallantly escorted her around and treated her to home-cooked meals that were finger-licking good. By now they were deeply in love. From the very beginning Onler seemed to understand the role he was destined to play in her life. He was to be her morale booster, caregiver, and a mentor. When Mary was scheduled to go to US for her first world championship, tucked into her purse was a sum of only ₹1,500. Onler's heart brimmed over with love and concern. He approached members of the Kom community at Delhi, met up with MPs from Manipur, and soon handed her a sum of ₹15,000. The couple, deeply committed to each other, had to go without the normal pleasures of dating and romance. Mary was totally focused on her burgeoning career, and Onler quietly played the role of being her strength. In 2005, Onler and Mary got married. She looked radiant in her white gown and frothy lace veil, her arm linked to her groom's. Many of her detractors made smug predictions that her career would take a nose dive, but the feisty bride, with the warm, all-embracing love of her husband, was poised for even more spectacular feats.

That same year, she won gold at the Asian Women's Championship in Taiwan and surged to victory at the AIBA Women's World Championship in Podolsk, Russia.

Then, in 2006, a heartrending tragedy befell the family. Onler's father, a 67-year-old school teacher, was brutally gunned down by a little-known group called Manipur Komrem National Front. A note next to his bloodied corpse informed that he had been given the capital punishment for working against the group. Till date, Onler is certain that the heinous murder is the work of vindictive suitors whom Mary had previously rejected. She was so traumatized by the murder of her gentle father-in-law that she even thought of bidding goodbye to her boxing career. But Onler would have none of it. Life, he said, would have to go on as before.

A few months later, the couple experienced a double blessing, as their twin boys were born. Mary had a difficult childbirth, and the babies were delivered by caesarean section. From being a world champion pugilist, Mary was now breastfeeding, washing nappies, and singing her boys to sleep. Mary thought it was the end of her career. But just a year afterwards, she wore her gloves and was raring to go. Her parents were very worried and feared that her caesarean stitches would rupture if someone punched her in the belly. Though Mary assured them there was no cause for concern, she was dismayed to find that her body lacked its old strength and suppleness. She tired easily, grow breathless, and her limbs ached as she drove herself to perform. But she resisted and was poised for a comeback. But it was heartbreaking for her to part from her twin

boys, Rechungver and Khupneivar. Thousands of miles away, trying to sleep in her hotel room, she would weep at the memory of
their baby prattle, their angelic smiles, and the way they loved to
bounce in her lap. But she had not come far along this lonely path
to turn back. Psyching herself to control her emotions, Mary forged
ahead with a trail of glory. She not only won the national championship but also the silver at the Asian Women's Championship
in Guwahati in 2008. Late that year, she got back her crown at
AIBA Women's World Championship in Ninspo, China.

***

Mary and Onler will always remember the year 2011 as one of
the bleakest in their lives. Their son Nainei was found by doctors to have a hole in his heart. He would have to be rushed to
Chandigarh's Postgraduate Institute of Medical Education and
Research. Onler persuaded Mary to leave for China as scheduled.
Mary won the gold medal and rushed back to be with her ailing
son. He was successfully operated on, and the couple breathed a
sigh of relief.

Mary's winning streak continued. In 2012, she won the gold medal
in the 51-kg class at the Asian Women's Boxing Championship in
Mongolia. For the record, in 2010, she had won the gold medal
at the Asian Women's Boxing Championship in Kazakhstan and
the AIBA Women's World Boxing Championship in Barbados,
her fifth consecutive gold in the championship. In the 2010 Asian
Games she competed in the 51-kg class and won a bronze medal.
Women's boxing is not included in the Commonwealth Games,
but Mary, along with fellow boxer Vijender Singh, had the honor
of bearing the Queen's baton in its opening ceremony.

The thin, shabbily dressed girl, whose eyes gleamed with mute
appeal so many years ago, was now an international star. The government had given her a job in the police force. There were armed

guards protecting her government quarters; trophies and medals jostled for space in her glass cases. The Indian government honored her with an Arjuna Award in 2004, the Padmashree in 2006, and the Rajiv Gandhi Khel Ratna in 2009. Mary could afford the best things of life. She loved to shop and give herself manicures. But when she was at home she loved to be just a mother and a wife, cooking, washing, cleaning, and playing with her boys. It was a time when she could relax, as no cameras beamed on her every move. Back at Kangethei, her parents and siblings got on with their simple lifestyle, happy to go on as before, unaffected by her fame and success. Looking at them, one is reminded of Mary's humble roots and the tremendous willpower and faith that took her this far. Her home state is on the periphery of mainstream India. Young Manipur boys and girls, venturing to the metros for studies and jobs, are called "chinkies" and mistaken for Chinese. These youths are compelled to migrate because Manipur has been in a permanent state of siege. There were as many as 32 rebel groups—breakaway factions clamoring for autonomy but without any consensus in the state. In the Manipur capital Imphal, wire barricades guard government buildings, and army flag marches are a daily affair, while the insurgents go on killing and extortion sprees, even children are kidnapped and forced to become child soldiers. The excesses of the insurgents have led to the imposition of the AFSPA, which gives the armed forces the power to arrest, interrogate, and even torture anyone at will.

In order to understand Mary, and the extraordinary power that propels her forward, we must know the desperation of her people, their struggle to lead a normal life, and the many odds they have to face.

There was a time when Mary was terrified of talking to her boxing coach when she met him for the first time, because, according to her, he looked like Mike Tyson. Now, as the years passed by, and she rose to the height of fame, she grew confident and articulate, addressing large gatherings as well as giving television interviews. She held center stage at a global investor summit. Dressed in a smart black blazer, cream pants, and enormous wedges, she talked about "Lessons from my journey" in her open, natural style, punctuating her sentences with girlish laughter. She switched now and then from English to Hindi. She said, "Boxing is a punishment game. You win, you get hurt. You lose, you get hurt," which was greeted with loud applause. She described how her passport and documents got stolen during one of her early trips abroad and how she prayed and agonized over whether to come back or stay. With heartwarming candor, she described how she was pummeled in the first bout of an Asian championship. She said, "I want to win every time, but I guess it's not possible." She then went on to say, "It's easy to perform well after marriage. The real challenge came later. I had to work very hard and have great willpower. When I gave birth to my sons, people said, 'It's over for Mary Kom.' I proved them wrong. Then in the Olympics, I had to play in the 51-kg category. I had played in the 46 and 48 kg only previously. My fellow sportsmen said unkind things behind my back. I don't fight them outside. I just want them to face me in the ring. When other contestants fight me and lose, they look upon me as the enemy. They don't consider it as only a game. I am proud to represent my state." Then she talks about creating new Olympic champions, new Mary Koms, in the future through her boxing academy.

However, it was Mary's success at the London Olympics and winning a medal for India that catapulted her to stratospheric heights. Her success is all the more significant because it was in 2012 that women's boxing was included in the Olympics for the first time. Yet, right at the very beginning Mary stared dismayed at what seemed an insurmountable obstacle. The lowest admitted weight in the Olympic Games was 51 kg. Mary had won one silver and five gold world championship titles only in the now defunct pin-weight (below 46 kg) and light flyweight (45–48 kg) categories. Her weight was clearly below the mandatory 51 kg. She drew comfort solely from the fact that she had once boxed in the 51-kg flyweight category at the 2010 Asian Games in Guangzhou, China, and bagged a bronze.

***

London, August 2012—Mary is in the ring, slugging it out with adversaries who are taller and heavier. But what works on her side is her in-built aggression, nimble footwork, and sheer staying power. First she defeated Karolina Michalezuk of Poland 19–14 and then demolished Maroua Rahali of Tunisia 15–6 in the quarterfinals. In the semifinals she met her old adversary Nicola Adams of Great Britain, who had routed her in a world championship in China, at the 10–12 AIBA Women's World Boxing Championship. As Nicola defeated Mary (6–11) the whole of India grieved for the feisty little warrior and understood her pain as she tearfully apologized for not being able to bring the gold. But the bronze was hers, an astonishing feat for a woman who had become a mother only a year before; a woman who hailed from a remote, backward, and trouble-torn state; and the daughter of an impoverished family. Indeed, she was Magnificent Mary, an icon of female empowerment, whose life was a saga of being able to make miracles possible. In fact, she says she is lucky to have been born poor, for it taught her to struggle hard and channelize her angst.

***

Filmmaker Sanjay Leela Bhansali is all set to make a biopic on Mary, with Priyanka Chopra essaying her role. Mary loves to sing Hindi songs and jokes that maybe, just maybe, the Manipuri rebels would lift the ban on Bollywood films after the movie on her.

   Mary is generously open about her fighting strategies. She says she tries to avoid distractions and keeps an eye on her strengths and weaknesses. Remembering the hardships she herself had to face in her quest to play this sport, in 2007, she set up the M.C. Mary Kom Boxing Academy at her home in Imphal's Langol Games Village. When Mary is at Imphal, she runs the whole show, and in her absence, Onler is in charge. She has no less than 30 students under her, one of whom has been the national champion, S. Nengneiket Kom. The academy has a large open field and some boxing gloves. There is no ring in which to practice. Fifteen of the students live with her. She even pays their school fees. She drives them hard. They rise at dawn, doing their warm-up exercises, running, jumping, shadow-boxing, and sparring. Working in pairs, trainees pummel their partners to focus. Through all this Mary's mongrels, Scuba and Steffi, bound around, barking in excitement. When Mary, after her own punishing morning work-out, comes to see how her students are doing; everybody perks up, putting in their best. Scowling, she moves among them, criticizing, encouraging, explaining, and making them titter with her mimicry of their moves. Mary herself was trained for the Olympics by her British coach Charles Atkinson, who taught her to be absolutely fearless when meeting her opponents head-on. He laid stress on building up her stamina and muscle mass for the event.

Mary's coaches believe that at 33, she will still be able to bag the gold or silver at the Rio Olympics in 2016. Recently having given birth to her third son, Mary looks forward to that distant date with quiet confidence and humility. And she draws strength from her favorite passage from the Bible, Mathew 7:8, "Ask, and it shall be given you; seek, and ye shall find; knock, and it shall be opened into you." No wonder the two words this million-dollar champ uses most often are "full confidence."

9
Opening the Cage: Hasina Kharbhih

There is much more to Hasina Kharbhih than her exotic ancestry (a Muslim father and a Seng Khasi mother), her evocative name, and her heart-stopping smile. Her silky hair falling in waves over her shoulders, she is never still, typing messages on her cell phone, chiding a niece for some minor act, consulting with her colleagues on some work detail, all the while tucking into an authentic Assamese *thali* of *khar*, *pitika*, and *masor tenga*. This petite 40-year-old is poised and articulate, a celebrity in her own right, the word celebrity in her case having none of its usual vapid and frivolous connotation.

"In my travels abroad, I have been mistaken for a Mexican, a Brazilian, a Filipino, even a Red Indian. My parents met at the international border between India and East Pakistan, when my maternal grandmother went to trade there. My Pakistani father made a passport for my mother, and she went to see his home and meet his family, so that she could make up her mind about marrying him. She came back and told him that 'it was he who would have to stay in India as her husband.'" So, Sukur Muhammad left his country behind for Kristilian Kharbhih, his Khasi sweetheart. He set up a farm at Balat, and gave shelter to many refugees from East Pakistan who had nowhere to go. "In fact, when I was born in 1971, Bangladesh was created, and these people left for their homes there. They blessed me as the harbinger of good news, and an old woman predicted that one day I would work among many people. Perhaps what I am doing today is a fulfillment of that prediction," she says.

True, you have to just Google Hasina Kharbhih's name to know just how much she has packed into her short life. She is the founder president and team leader of Impulse NGO Network, a social organization working in the field of child trafficking, HIV/AIDS intervention, and livelihood-support initiatives for rural Northeast India. She is the brain behind the internationally recognized Meghalaya Model, a comprehensive tracking system that has been developed out of the collaboration of state government and security agencies, legal groups, media, and citizen organizations to combat cross-border trafficking of children in India's porous Northeast.

Not surprisingly, the general public is not very aware of the implications of human trafficking. Trafficking in persons is a serious crime and a grave violation of human rights. It refers to the act of recruiting, transporting, transferring, harboring, or receiving a person through the use of force, coercion, or other means, for the purpose of exploiting them. Every year thousands of men, women, and children fall into the clutches of traffickers, both in their own countries as well as abroad.

Human trafficking, especially child trafficking, has shown an alarming upward trend in this region in present years and the reasons are not far to seek. Isolated both by geography and politics, the Northeast is torn apart by ethnic unrest and separatist movements. People have been displaced from their homes, law-enforcing agencies have their hands full trying to apprehend terrorists, and a population beleaguered by poverty, illiteracy, and unemployment, all are flash points that have led to this situation. Worse, the region has a porous international border with Myanmar, Bangladesh, and

Bhutan, a boon for gangs of traffickers to move their victims with impunity.

Traffickers exploit this unstable environment to lure families into sending their children to cities to work. Trafficking syndicates are flooding the area with offers of modeling jobs, work in beauty parlors, and call centers. Hasina's Impulse NGO Network conducted a study and found that the highways in Meghalaya made it easy for prostitution to flourish. The clients are invariably truck drivers from Punjab, Haryana, Uttar Pradesh, Bihar, and so on. Unfortunately, the governments have not regarded checking this crime as a priority, and the police lack the data and the infrastructure to take effective steps. There is lack of communication and coordination between the police forces of different states. There is also no mechanism to monitor recruitment agencies.

Rehabilitation of these victims is a daunting task. The legal system is underdeveloped, and there are major language barriers. There are no facilities for post-recovery counseling and rehabilitation schemes.

Looking deep into this problem in all its ramifications, Hasina got to work. She decided to work with the National Human Rights Commission to include secondary data from all the Northeastern states: Assam, Manipur, Sikkim, Arunachal Pradesh, and primary data from the two most vulnerable states of Assam and Meghalaya. She presented her study at the National Action Against Trafficking and Sexual Exploration of Children Network Consultation in Kolkata. This helped her to connect with organizations working on this issue all over the country, thereby leading to the creation of the Meghalaya Model. At the same time, she reactivated the defunct State Committee on Human Trafficking. What then is the Meghalaya Model? In simple terms, it is a formal collaboration between different agencies of the state government, law enforcement, lawyers, and a national network of organizations working on trafficking in the country. The model's aim is to track and rescue children in the sex trade, facilitate rehabilitation, provide families

with livelihood alternatives, prosecute offenders, and raise awareness on the issue.

"It is like this," explains Hasina earnestly. "The model's start-off
point is a weekly outreach program for children at various sourcing
points run by volunteers. The volunteers spend time with the children, discuss their needs, and teach them about their basic rights.
The children are also given nutritional supplements and nonformal
education through extracurricular activities. Thus, a data bank is
created for each child, and this helps us to keep track of his/her
whereabouts. Children also reveal valuable information on the fly-
by-night operators, their modus operandi, and other missing children. It works within the 5 Ps—Prevention, Protection, Policing,
Press, and Persecution, and the 3 Rs—Rescue, Rehabilitation, and
Repatriation."

"As you can see, communication and information sharing are
vital tools in tackling this menace. So Impulse NGO Network
uses the Internet to connect the different stakeholders. We launch
e-mail campaigns and web alerts to spread information among
partner organizations and post updated information and photos
of missing children and the history of rescued children. The state
police are able to use these data to ensure quick action."

"But then, we have to think of the post-rescue scenario. So we
have pushed for government funding for shelter homes—where
counselors work with rescued children. They monitor the child's
progress for a year after the rescue, to make sure he/she does not
fall into the trap again. If a child does not wish to return to the
family, Impulse coordinates with other organizations to shelter the
child and provide education and livelihood. Our NGO counselors
are working with all agencies in order to formalize a system of
information collection from rescued girls."

"So," Hasina says emphatically, "the Meghalaya Model is aimed
at combating child trafficking in Northeast India as a single, comprehensive, strategic plan, to be adopted by all state agencies and
citizen organizations in the region and in the nearby crossings to

Bhutan, China, Myanmar, Thailand, and Bangladesh. It enables governments and citizen groups to jointly implement the 3 Ps—Prevention, Protection, and Persecution, and the 3 Rs—Rescue, Relief, and Rehabilitation. The different actors communicate and share data more effectively and use the same training manuals, standard operating procedures, and public awareness campaign. A legal support network, which includes a victim protection program, identifies and reports on traffickers. An anti-trafficking course is being integrated into the curriculum of Police Training Schools to create child-friendly systems. We have also created a Helpline Resource Directory of the region, which was developed by the Social Welfare Department of Meghalaya. It has been approved by the Indian government and supported by the United Nations. I work directly with the state government and government agencies to make sure that the model is fully absorbed in their operations instead of being merely linked. I am very happy to tell you that the Meghalaya Model has been tested to be effective and it is one of the best-practice models included in the South Asian Regional Initiative/Equity Study by Management System International in Washington, D.C., and supported by United States Agency for International Development (USAID) for replication in South East Asia."

Interviewing Hasina, I get the impression that here indeed is a focused, determined, and fiercely independent woman who knows exactly where she is going. But as she gradually opens up to me, I sense that behind the façade is a sensitive woman scarred by a marriage gone sour. Quietly, and precisely, Hasina sums up the person she is. "I am normally a calm and patient person," she says. "But when I find out that someone is lying to me, it unleashes a lot of anger. I cannot bear any form of deception," she says. She is also somewhat of a perfectionist. She likes her room arranged in a certain way. Being a neatness freak, her office is always in perfect order. "I am a bit old-fashioned when it comes to certain superstitions. I spit three times when a black cat crosses my path," she says.

"You want to know about my faith? Well, Dad was Muslim and my mother a Seng Khasi. Her forefathers have worshipped the sun, the moon, and the stars. There are many Hindu elements in her faith. I read the Koran and can write Arabic. My dad always said religion was a matter of personal choice. I myself am drawn to the teaching of the Buddha."

You may be under the impression that all Hasina does is work. That is not entirely true. She enjoys dressing up. "I had been, in fact, done a spot of modeling in my college days. I had done ad campaigns and featured in cover shoots. Impulse Social Enterprise has undertaken research on our traditional textiles. I always make it a point to wear ethnic outfits when I attend seminars and workshops abroad," she says. She enjoys traveling and seeing new places. "My pleasures are simple, like walking to and from work. I enjoy cooking, especially Mughlai dishes like biryani, kebabs, and kormas. I pick up recipes during my travels abroad. I bring guests home instead of taking them to a restaurant," she adds. Family is very important to her. She is very close to her siblings as well as her nieces and nephews. "It is very fortunate to have a large, loving family as your support system," she adds. At last Hasina is ready to talk about her troubled past. Drawing a deep breath, she says, "I got married in 2006. We were brought together by our families. But barely six months later, we were separated. You cannot share your life with an alcoholic. I moved heaven and earth to make him sober—counseling, attending Alcoholic Anonymous meets, you name it, I did it. I soon realized that I was more a counselor than a wife. I returned to my mother's house. But I continued to try and change him. But then, when we faced each other in court, he said I was ambitious, obsessed about my own career, and that I did not want children. I was made to look like the villain. Along with fighting the case, I was also building up my NGO. Certain people who were against my work used my divorce to attack me. This ordeal made me see life in all its dark shades, and I grew up pretty fast. I realized that when a marriage breaks up, it is always the woman who is blamed. But I have not given up on love. For the last four years I am seeing someone and it is a very fulfilling relationship. I have met so many people, but when I met my partner, I instantly knew he was the one. We respect and support each other."

Looking back, had Hasina always had this dream to bring in change in the society she lived in? "Yes, I was involved with a school charity group, of which I became an active member. Then I created an alumni network. In college I began to work in a crafts village close to my ancestral village, providing design inputs and introducing their craft to new markets, even abroad. It has now evolved into a full-fledged livelihood program for helping craftspersons to connect to new markets through export of their products. As I began to train volunteers for the village program, things began to take a distinct focus. I realized the need of the youth to talk about issues close to them but which were seldom acknowledged by society. Sexual health lessons and other related issues such as AIDS and drugs counseling were included in our interactions. The Meghalaya government now runs it in 60 schools. It was from this program that I began to look at the problem of child trafficking. We took the children trekking and discussed issues relating to AIDS and sexuality. We also had a Magic Box in class where children put questions anonymously, to be later answered by teachers."

I was curious to know how the Meghalaya Model worked to help children who are victims of trafficking. Hasina explains, "The process begins with the reporting of a missing child. This is reported to Impulse or one of our partners through a child's parents or relative, partner NGOs, organizations, individuals, media, or the police. Once a report has been made to Impulse, the information is sent to all our national partners such as ATSEC, CACT, and so on and Impulse uses a web alert to contact and conduct a follow-up with the police. Then a first information report (FIR) is filed by Impulse or the partner organizations, depending on the location of the missing child or Impulse assists family members to file an FIR."

"The next part of the process deals with the rescue. When a partner organization conducts a raid with the help of the police, either as a result of information provided by Impulse or information that they have received themselves, Impulse is contacted to confirm whether the rescued survivors are from the Northeast. In the meantime, the child is provided temporary shelter. The trafficked survivor is brought to Impulse or our state partners, escorted by law enforcement or Child Welfare Committee if the victim is under 18 years of age. The next steps involve repatriation and rehabilitation. Hopefully, the final stage is prosecution. Impulse will file an FIR or help the family to file an FIR."

At this point Hasina clarifies, "Meghalaya is home to possibly the world's largest surviving matrilineal culture, and yet, this does not act as a deterrent to trafficking. The matrilineal system does not control, or even curb, human trafficking in Meghalaya. Although women used to enjoy a special status within it, this system is not a matriarchy. A unique aspect of the matrilineal system is that the youngest daughter inherits the family wealth and property; however, she must act as its guardian rather than its sole possessor. Any decision regarding the inheritance needs to be passed to the maternal uncle. Power has generally remained in the hands of men, both within the clan and family. We still cannot take part in rituals, and it is only now that we are allowed to attend clan meetings."

Hasina started her work at a very early age and had to deal with the skepticism of people around her. This only made her resolve to strive harder and she set up a punishing schedule of work. Slowly, painstakingly, she developed the contacts and methodology to combat human trafficking. Inevitably she earned the wrath of criminal gangs whose business was affected by her vigilante activism.

With a rueful smile she reveals, "I've faced threats, attacks while dealing with this issue, especially when putting traffickers behind bars. Threatening calls are not unusual in my line of work but it got really serious in 2008. In that year recruitment agencies luring young women had sprung up overnight all across the region. They offered jobs in private airlines, the hotel industry, and as tour operators. Young women who had just completed school were interviewed in closed hotel rooms and promised free education and free jobs abroad. We found that the agencies were looking for all the things that a modeling agency would look for, except that these were not modeling agencies. Parents started telling us about their daughters who had gone away to work, never to return. Some said they were put into massage parlors and forced into prostitution."

"The calls started as I began to dig deeper into what was going on. For instance, I received threats from a man and a woman; the man called each time from a different mobile and the woman called each time from a different PCO, both asking me to call back to one mobile number. The caller would say, 'Stop investigating the recruitment agencies, especially the one from Goa or face the consequences.'"

"'Hello Hasina, you are in a restaurant right now. You are wearing such and such a dress. You are sitting with three people'; they knew my whereabouts. It continued for weeks. I filed an FIR, mentioning the phone numbers and the kind of threats I was getting. That was September 2008."

"I went to the police station after a fortnight, to know what they had found out. They told me that one of the holders of the phone number I had given had come to take anticipatory bail. In Meghalaya, the anticipatory bail is given by the district council in tribal versus tribal cases, but not in criminal cases. Surprisingly, she was given bail. I soon found out that she was among the list of girls recruited by a private airlines and she was working at a bungalow in Goa as an escort girl."

"The investigation officer was transferred within 15 days. The second investigation officer took medical leave for two months.

This continued for a year. My chargesheet was never filed by the police. Later, another young girl from Meghalaya was arrested in Bangalore airport for drug trafficking. We were contacted by the Bangalore police and the media to check whether she was a victim of human trafficking. We found out that she was on the same list as the girl who had got the anticipatory bail and was her friend. The girls who had escaped from Goa gave us the list. They told us how the final interview takes place in the residence of the boss in Mumbai. With a glass of beer in his hand, he would invite each girl to work in his house and his airlines. The girls organized numerous parties in his residence, take care of his guests, and also act as personal escorts. When I gave the media this information, I was charged with defamation against the girl who was one of the callers threatening me, and an arrest warrant was issued against me a day before it would expire, and hence, I would barely get time to get bail."

"In May 2009 I was assaulted outside the court. Caught in the traffic, late for a hearing, I walked to the district court premises. When crossing the busy road to get to the entrance, I was pushed dangerously close to the trucks passing by. One man, two girls, and two women from Goa had been threatening me. They followed me inside, pushing, abusing—the woman scratched my arm. Somehow I got away and called the police. 'File an FIR,' they said. But the police cannot arrest anyone in the court premises, so that didn't happen either. Half an hour later, a journalist informed me that the same girl was now holding a press conference claiming that I had tried to strangle her. Next day, the local newspapers ran a headline 'Human rights defender Hasina Kharbhih assaults a girl.' I didn't know what to do. At one point in the press conference she described herself as a pilot escort girl, but nobody once thought of asking what she meant."

The state government said I had a problem with the girl because I was going through a divorce. Nothing ever came of the special investigation they conducted. As she shrugs her slim shoulder dismissively, I ask her if she has any regrets. "Absolutely not," she replies firmly. "Right from my school days I have enjoyed volunteering in various activities. The Leadership Training Service at St. Joseph's school, Shillong, inculcated the spirit of active participation. My friends and I debated for long hours how we could bring in change and what we could set right in the world around us. When we passed out of school, we wanted to continue this and came up with the idea of starting the LTS Alumni, which in course of time led to the formation of the Impulse NGO Network. I wanted to prove that though we were young, we were capable of getting things done and making a difference. I am a person who takes things positively, no matter how tough the circumstances are. I am a total workaholic because I simply love what I do. As a social entrepreneur, I am married to my vision and I cannot rest until I achieve my goals. My focus is on protecting children because they have no say in their rights. In these long and often challenging years, my biggest success has been in the replication of the Meghalaya Model in eight Northeastern states and its being under review for national replication. The model has managed to scale up when I was elected as an Ashoka Fellow in 2006. Ashoka Innovation for the public recognized that my idea can bring in wider change, and it helped me devote full time to the process. I am proud of having moved to a different level. Through fellowships, awards, and the support of the public, my determination to make a difference stands rock solid. Another success I am proud of it is the implementation of the handbook for law enforcement in all the police training schools of the eight Northeastern states, including Northeast Police Academy, and various other academies in the country."

Hasina is geared to facilitate long-term preventive measures to stop human trafficking. A new endeavor has been made to provide livelihood initiatives through Impulse Social Enterprises, which she founded in 2001 and represents as its managing director.

It is, according to her, a social mission–driven company comprising various brands, products, and services.

Hasina speak eloquently about the phenomenon of human trafficking. "Within this beautiful, yet tiny pocket of the world, the buying and selling of people generates a lucrative trade. Almost 98 percent of the region is connected to international borders with Bangladesh, Bhutan, China, and Myanmar. This geopolitical location is highly conducive to human trafficking. Truck drivers use the highways to trade drugs, whereas armed conflict and oppressive social structures are responsible for trafficking in all the Northeastern states. Poverty and ethnic violence are significant factors. Thousands of men, women, and children fall victim to it. Trafficking occurs both across borders and within India to destinations including New Delhi, Mumbai, Pune, Goa, and Kolkata and extends as far as to Thailand, Singapore, and Malaysia. There are equal numbers for sexual exploitation and labor trafficking. Children are vulnerable as they are viewed as the cheapest source of labor. Those sexually exploited run a high risk for HIV/AIDS due to the wide prevalence of the myth that sex with a minor can cure AIDS. Investigations into Northeast's trafficking scene started emerging only after a child labor survey was conducted in 2002. We, at Impulse, found unexplainably large numbers of missing women in Indian villages bordering Nepal and Bangladesh. The briskness of human trafficking slowly became evident, and more thoroughly explored, thanks to accounts of rescued survivors and interviews with family members. We have found Siliguri to be the main transit point. It connects many train lines and bus services. Women and children have been thus smuggled across the Indo-Nepal border."

"The poor fall easy victims. But a new trend has emerged whereby young, educated girls seeking employment outside their local area have been caught up in this racket. They are duped or coerced into the sex trade. NRIs have fraudulently married women and kept them as domestic help. The usual price offered for a victim differs. It differs depending on the age, the brothel buying the women/children, where the destination point is, the purpose intended for the victim, how young/pretty she is, and her education (ability to converse in English is a plus point). Generally speaking, the price ranges from ₹15,000 to ₹30,000 in the flesh market (US$300–US$600), whereas child laborers are sold to the middlemen at ₹5,000 to ₹7,000 (US$100–US$140). They are put to work in appalling conditions. If you are a victim you have no control over your body, no ability to say 'no' or 'that's enough.' You are no longer human, but a slave. There is no free will and you are just an object. Trafficked victims are sold again and again. They do not have rights to their earnings. They are repeatedly violated, brutalized, maimed, humiliated, and undergo physical and psychological trauma. Trafficked victims endure sadistic punishments such as beatings, cigarette burnings, and insertion of chili into the private parts."

Hasina carries her work forward with a small band of like-minded individuals. Among them is Rosanna Lyngdoh, her classmate from Lady Keane College, who is also a board member and team leader at Impulse. Hasina's brother A.G. Kharbhih has rendered his services to Impulse NGO Network for the past 14 years, tending to the legal and financial aspects. Rosanna has implemented projects, conducted training, and undertaken research and surveys. Besides she has also been active in field work, taking up family studies and helping out in returning children to their parents. Accounts Manager Debotosh Purkayastha, and E. Chen, the Administration Manager, complete the team. Volunteers from all over the country and abroad offer their services to both Impulse NGO Network and Impulse Social Enterprises.

The future is filled with challenges. Tossing back her hair, Hasina doodles on a paper napkin and explains, "We are on a plan to empower the people and to do that there is a core strategy. First, we have to remove the middlemen between the producers and the market. Then, we are making efforts to foster corporate social responsibility, which encourages investment in products that do well. We are also increasing production and income for artisans who had previously limited access to the market. Our target for the next three years is to reach 20,000 artisans in eight Northeastern states of India. Impulse Social Enterprises mobilizes artisans in villages to become independent entrepreneurs. Our team provides designers, marketing, and engages local partners along with artisans to create Impulse 2 Empower—a product line consisting of various textile products. The artisans thus have access to international markets, fair wages, fair trade, and the freedom of running their own business. Think of what it would mean—better education, better homes, good health, and proper nutrition. Our products include tablemats, bags, lampshades, scarves, and in addition to the product promotion, we allow our end-users the opportunity to support important human rights causes, namely, anti-trafficking activities, and fair trade and fair wage work for at-risk communities in Northeast India."

"For more than 17 years, Impulse has been working with rural communities in Meghalaya to guide them to sustainable livelihood. The work with villages started in 1993 with the Syntein Village Project, utilizing local traditions with handicrafts and handiwork. We furthered the village adoption program by helping Laitsohum village. Then, the Development Commissioner Handicrafts, Ministry of Textiles, Government of India, New Delhi, chose Impulse as the implementing agency for a Babasaheb Ambedkar Hastshilp Vikas Yojana (AHVY) Project. We began the Shillong Common Facility Centre to expose our artisans to technology, designs, and training."

Hasina's work has opened many doors to her. From 2004 to 2007, she served as Commonwealth Youth Ambassador for Positive Living representing India and is now an active member of the organization's alumni. In 2006, she was featured as a Yuva Star or Young Achiever for the BBC World Service. She has featured in the award-winning production of *Haath Se Haath Milega*

(Lets join hands), India's largest HIV/AIDS Awareness mass media campaign that reached over 50 million viewers. In 2006, she was selected as an Ashoka Fellow for conceiving the Meghalaya Model.

Today Hasina Kharbhih's work has spread far beyond her own land. As she says, "Human trafficking is an international problem, and so there must be an international approach. The Look East Policy opens the Indian borders toward the east; while this process will benefit many people, creating new opportunities for international business cooperation and movement, it also increases the opportunities for cross-border criminal activities, including human trafficking. There is a need for vigil against this."

Many years ago Hasina and her band of friends began their journey by excitedly bringing in chairs, tables, cushions, racks, and posters to set up their office. With stars in their eyes they dreamt of bringing changes in the community, protecting its most vulnerable from those who tried to rob them of their innocence and debase and oppress them. But Hasina is not one to bask in the glow of her success; she must be in the thick of action, as she always has been.

10

Woman on the Go:
Monisha Behal

At the unearthly hour of 6:00 am in the morning, a petite woman closes the windows of her Guwahati flat, zips her small suitcase, slings her tote bag on one shoulder, grabs the car keys, and is ready to go. Dressed in pea green trousers and a canary yellow T-shirt, Dr Monisha Behal, or Ben *Baideo* to all, is youthful and vivacious, looking much younger than her 62 years. Her movements, like her words, are economical.

"Hop in," she says as she turns on the ignition of her Sumo. Soon we are bowling down the highway at 80 miles per hour, making the most of the light traffic and the coolness of the cloudy monsoon weather. Our destination is Tezpur, a town 175 km northeast of Guwahati, an ancient city considered the cultural capital of the state. We are on our way to Jonak, Monisha's ancestral home, the place where, surrounded by the memorabilia of the past, Monisha unwinds and plays the piano, plays "Fetch" with Nupi, her beloved Labrador-boxer when she is not globetrotting, attending seminars, exhorting women to take charge of their lives, or trying to get justice for a wronged victim; Monisha loves to be here, where her life started.

Three hours later Monisha, who has been wearing a waist brace to protect her back, expertly steers the Sumo in through the grounds of Jonak. I take in the sight of the sprawling three-storied yellow-painted house flanked by tall trees and flowering shrubs. It has a pleasant unkempt feel; the lawn has not been mowed, and the creepers run riotously all around. On the first floor, a semicircular balcony is ringed with inviting wicker chains. The living room has low windows on three sides. Above the brick-color fireplace are photographs of her parents. There are sepia-tinted photographs on all sides, and on a corridor mounted innocuously on the wall, is Indira Gandhi's letter to Monisha's aunt, the late Neera Dogra. "I am so sorry I have not been able to see as much of you as I would like," Mrs Gandhi wrote. "Life is so rushed; one has hardly any time for friends." The letter is dated July 11, 1971.

I am to spend two days with Monisha, going through the story of her life and what made her arguably the most visible and vocal women's activist in this part of the country. She has been described as one of the pioneers of the NGO movement in the Northeast, one who has structured and professionalized social work, with fortuitous results. She is the founder member and chairperson of the North East Network (NEN). NEN is a women's rights organization working in the Northeast, with a focus on women's human rights. It acts as a facilitator to embark Northeast women on livelihood, health, conflict governance through capacity building, awareness raising, networking research, and advocacy. It works to ensure women's participation at all levels.

For her proactive role in working tirelessly for the cause of women's upliftment, Dr Monisha Behal has been honored with the Annanya Award by Lok Sabha Speaker Sri Somnath Chatterjee on March 9, 2007. It is an award constituted by the Ministry of Women and Child Development. Earlier, in 2004, she was given the Sanskriti Award for Outstanding Social Achievement. In 2011, came the 7th Eastern India Women's Association Award for Social Work in 2011.

Monisha Behal often downplays her illustrious antecedents and feels nothing useful can come of playing out the glory of the past.

But, in order to understand her life's work and the ideals that drive her, it is necessary to know about her family, and the larger-than-life characters who continue to inhabit the cultural space of Assam. Monisha is the niece of Jyoti Prasad Agarwala, noted Assamese playwright, songwriter, poet, writer, and filmmaker. A cultural icon even during his lifetime, he is idolized for his creative vision and is called the Rupkonwar of Assamese culture. He made the first Assamese film, *Joymoti*, in 1935, when Indian cinema was in its infancy. Jyoti Prasad himself was the nephew of another illustrious litterateur, Chandra Kumar Agarwala. The family patriarch Nabagram Agarwala had come to Assam in 1811 from the Marwar region in Rajasthan. The family acquired two tea estates—Bholaguri and Tamulbari. During the struggle for independence, the family home at Poki was visited by national leaders like Gandhiji and Pandit Nehru. In 1932 Jyoti Prasad Agarwala was jailed for his activities in the struggle for independence from the British rule. In 1942, he went underground to escape British repression. Toward the end of his life, he arrived at a radical vision, very different from the Romanticism of the early years.

Monisha was deeply influenced by two women of the immediate family, her mother Padma Agarwala and aunt Meena Agarwala. The wise and gentle Padma gave her equal freedom as her brothers and never forced her into rituals and customs she could not relate to. From her Monisha picked up the skills of empathizing with all kinds of people, skills that would stand her good stead in her life's mission.

An equally important role was played by aunt Meena Agarwala. Guided by the Gandhian principles of self-reliance, truth, and non-violence, she took over the reins of Tezpur Mahila Samiti from her mother-in-law Kironmoyee Agarwala; the organization helps countless people at the time of floods, earthquakes, riots, and war. In her quietly efficient way, she marshaled the local housewives to undertake projects in handloom, weaving, sericulture, textile

production, besides health care, family welfare, and thrift coopera-
tives. The Tezpur District Mahila Samiti (TDMS) was set up in
1928; on the advice of Gandhiji, it was given a fresh lease of life by
Meena Agarwala in the 1940s when she came in as the bride of the
Agarwala family. Her work had a ripple effect, and similar bodies
grew up all over the state. She was honored with the Janaki Devi
Bajaj Award in 1998 for her services. Remarkable women like
Kironmoyee Agarwala, Chandraprabha Saikiani, Chandrabala
Barua, Padma Agarwala, and Hemlata Barua built the edifice of
the TDMS.

The little girl Monisha, tousle-haired and curious as a cat, would
hang out at the office of the TDMS, listening to the women talking at the meetings, someone counting money, another at the
loom, and yet another counseling a woman in distress. There was
no time for idle chatter; arguments broke out, but matters were
swiftly sorted out. Day by day, as Monisha grew up, she had a
ringside view about how a women's cooperative worked and all
its strengths and weaknesses. She did not know it then, but she too
had a role waiting to be taken up in the coming future.

As mentioned earlier, Monisha, the youngest daughter of
Hridayanath and Padma Agarwala, had the legendary Jyoti Prasad
Agarwala as her paternal uncle. She says she has no memories of
him, as he had passed away in her infancy. The legacy of this first
family of Assamese culture sits lightly on her. "I find no reason to
harp on the fact that I am Jyoti Prasad Agarwala's niece. I would
rather concentrate on my own contribution to society. But of
course I realize, in retrospect, that growing up with this family
gave me some unique advantages. We grew up in a liberal household where our freedom was respected. We were taught to see
things in the larger context of India. My father's elder sister was
Neera Dogra, who later became Chairman, Central Social Welfare
Board. Every evening we went to Poki, the stately family home
and played noisy, delightful games. When we got too raucous,

the elders herded us to the Jonaki cinema hall that our uncle Jyoti Prasad built in 1937, and all of us cousins and siblings had a wonderful time watching movies like *Paigam*."

"I do not have a single memory of violence or unhappiness in my childhood. Knowing my interest in cars and bikes, dad encouraged me to drive around and also took me to fishing. Ma always took me to the TDMS where I saw women discussing issues, weaving clothes, and keeping records and all that."

"Ma was a very giving person. She would also go to the Naamghar next to our house and interact with the women there, praying with them and sharing their problem. Ours was an open house, with poets, artists, singers, dancers, and freedom fighters trooping in at all hours of the day and night, and everybody was welcomed and accommodated. I remember *jalsa*s or performances in which the legendary Bhupen Hazarika sang late into the night."

"So ours was a joyous, free-flowing childhood. We rode on the branches of coconut palms, dragging them along the ground, and made tops out of match sticks and litchi seeds. There was no opulence as such, and we had to make do with what we had. I was very unhappy and, therefore, had to be packed off to a boarding school—Loreto Convent in Darjeeling. Though the views of the Himalayas were spectacular and I learned to play the piano, I missed my home dreadfully. I missed the chaotic pleasure of looking after the cows, chicken, and goats, and my visits to the Naamghar and Mahila Samiti and to Poki to meet my cousins."

"More than anything else, my upbringing made me a people person. We learnt how important it was to get along with people. I remember how Ma never wore jewelry when she went to the Naamghar, thus making herself one of the simple women. The Mahila Samiti taught me that women could have a life beyond the home and the kitchen."

Monisha's real initiation into her path of life came when she moved from the rather elite Loreto Convent in Darjeeling to Delhi's Indraprastha College 1971 to study political science. Suddenly, people all around her were arguing passionately for social justice, equality, worker's rights, and Leftist ideology in 1971. It was the year Bangladesh was born, and India's military might seemed formidable. It was a heady time to be young and believe that the old order was on its way to make way for the new. Monisha was then living with her aunt, her father Hridayananda Agarwala's elder sister Neera Dogra, who was Chairman, Central Social Welfare Board. The formidable, hard-to-please aunt Neera left the young Monisha tongue-tied with her brisk, no-nonsense manner.

This was not to say that Monisha was subdued. She had many friends and was forever borrowing her male friends' bikes for hour-long rides. Tomboy was the word on everybody's tips when describing her, though she herself found the word demeaning.

Then, in 1977, Monisha married Rana Behal, an academician, and looked for a way to translate her ideals to action. One day she met Vina Mazumdar at the Centre for Women's Development Studies in Delhi and had a long chat about her foray into an ethnography project on the musical tradition of Northeast tribes. It was a portentous meeting. Dr Vina Mazumdar was an Indian academic, feminist, a scholar in women's studies in India, and a leading figure of the women's movement in post-independence India. She was among the first women academics to combine activism with scholarly research in women's studies. She was the founding director of the Centre for Women's Development Studies, an autonomous organization. A few days later, Vina had a proposal for her. The center was mooting the idea of a directory on women's cooperatives all over India. Could Monisha do the project for one district in Assam?

"So I came to Assam and started my work. I was assigned the Kamrup district. I was shocked to see how much women were discriminated against and denied their personal freedom and rights. The higher was the caste, the more were the women withdrawn from community life. In many cooperatives, the men held the posts, whereas the women were mere workers. Money and power were clearly in male hands. Vina Mazumdar gave me a lot of freedom, and I discovered new facets of the society I had been born into."

"Another highlight of those years was when Vina Mazumdar sent me to Ahmedabad to meet the legendary Ela Bhatt of SEWA. I had avidly read about this remarkable woman and how she was able to mobilize thousands of women in meaningful endeavors. A lawyer by training, Ela Bhatt initiated the Self-Employed Women's Association of India in 1972, which provided microfinance for child care, literacy programs, and legal assistance to more than 500,000 poor rural women." Monisha was able to see for herself the range of support programs and the sheer number of women being helped. She saw how Bhatt was able to organize and convince people, by example or the spoken word, toward a common, organizational goal. In spite of being a respected leader of the international labor, cooperatives, women's upliftment, and microfinance movements, Ela Bhatt came across as a simple, humble woman, without any awareness about her charisma.

"What was remarkable was that Ela was so ahead of her times. She made videos of her collaborative effort, so that it remained as a record and also as training material. Through her I learnt how vital it was for an organization to have a solid grip of its accounts. It was a joy to see how SEWA worked."

At around this time, Monisha avidly read a book that had a profound effect on her—*Behind Mud Walls*, authored by Charlotte Melina Viall Wiser and William H. Wiser, a true life account of this couple who arrived in India in 1925 and settled down in the North Indian village of Karimpur. Over the next five years, they wrote one of the first accounts of rural India originally published in 1930. Charlotte Wiser continued to observe and write from Karimpur till her death, when American anthropologist Susan Wadley picked up the narrative. With updates from the 1960s, 1970s, 1984, and 2000, this expanded edition encapsulates 75 years of continuity and change. In the 1980s, Monisha was roped in to assist in the project. Four decades after independence, Karimpur had seen many changes—changes in agriculture, labor relations, political structures, education, family, and gender relations. The original blueprints did not work anymore. The Karimpur villagers turn to their gods and goddesses to cope with a chaotic, uncaring world, says Monisha.

"I got the offer to assist her on her work in India. I spent months at Karimpur, in Mainpuri district in Uttar Pradesh, to write 13 case studies of women. It was a tremendous experience. The women were no better than cattle. They were confined to the inner court-yards, married off before attaining puberty, beaten for dowry, or for bearing a girl child. They had no access to money, health facilities, and education. At that time I had just completed my PhD dissertation on Vaishnavism. I admired the humaneness of Vaishnavism and its high regard for woman. And here, on the other hand, in the heart of so-called developed India, I came across women who were dehumanized to a shocking degree."

"After my stint at Karimpur, I decided to return to my roots. I had fond memories of my years observing my aunt Meena Agarwala and other women leaders organizing themselves and working to better the lives of women. Away from home, I had learnt much and gained valuable insight into the power of collaborative action. I wanted to contribute that knowhow in order to assist TDMS into getting funds and being more productive in their work."

"I interviewed my aunt Meena Agarwala, the women at the Samiti and wrote about them in the local media. I told the women it was time to garner funds for this organization. Such an effort had not been made before. The Samiti had had implicit belief in Gandhian volunteerism. I compiled a history of the Samiti and designed a project proposal. I then applied for the Foreign Contribution Regulation Act Certificate to the Home Ministry, and with that certificate we were able to get aid from Oxfam, USA. It was a great feeling to do something for an organization I had belonged to since I was a toddler."

"Now it was time for another move. I was beginning to develop a new confidence. Hadn't I walked up nine floors to get the Foreign Contribution Regulation Act (FCRA) Certificate? Hadn't I persuaded Americans to put in their dollars for a group in an obscure Indian town they had never heard about? So now I joined as the Gender Equity Adviser of the Canadian International Development Agency (CIDA). My brief was to advise them on which projects to fund."

The year 1995 was important in Monisha's life. She established the NEN during the mobilization process for the Beijing Conference. The United Nations convened the Fourth World Conference on Women, Action for Equity, Development and Peace in Beijing in the month of September. In order to understand better what NEN is all about, I talked to Anurita Hazarika, program manager. She says NEN is a women's rights organization working in the Northeast Region of India with a focus on women's human rights. It has acted as a facilitator to empower women on issues of livelihood, health, conflict, and governance through capacity building, awareness raising, networking, research, and advocacy. While Monisha is the chairperson and executive director, four small groups of men and women carry out the work from Guwahati, Chizami (in Nagaland), Shillong, and Delhi. Funding comes from contributions by governments, foundations, organizations, and individuals.

Over the years, NEN has systematically documented human rights violations of women in the region. These helped formulate policy interventions. It networks with women's organizations across the world and carries out advocacy at national and international platforms. It imparts training in working for women's issues and disseminates information critical to women's safety. NEN emphasizes that women's rights fall within the purview of human rights. Changing mindsets, from grassroots level to policy implementing levels, is the main focus of NENs advocacy work. NEN is focused on the following thematic areas: peace and conflict,

Convention to Eliminate All Forms of Discrimination Against Women (CEDAW), health, livelihood and crafts, national resource management, violence against women (VAW), and youth.

***

Her cellphone beeped. It was her husband Rana. There was genuine warmth and caring in Monisha's voice. I thought it fitting to ask her if she rated herself as a good wife. She answered with her trademark honesty. "I am not at all the traditional or the ideal wife. At home, it is Rana who can rustle up the gourmet meal or do the laundry. But I am organized and house-proud. I buy the things with which we decorate our house. We have shared the task of looking after our children Shyamant and Hiyamani. These days, they are in Goa and Paris, respectively. Rana is a teacher at Deshbandhu College, Delhi. I shuttle between Guwahati, Delhi, Tezpur, and Chizami in Nagaland. We both respect each other's work. That is so important. I have been an indulgent mother. I surrounded them with music. They have both turned out to be musicians. I played popular English and Assamese numbers to them on the piano and read them stories. There were many moments of guilt when I had to leave them on field trips."

For Monisha, the year 1995 was a fulfilling period in more than one way: She was awarded the prestigious MacArthur Fellowship. She chose to conduct a study of the health and economic status of women in two villages of seven districts of Nagaland. Always one to welcome adventure with open arms, Monisha had a cheerful disregard of the ground realities: the long-running battle between the insurgents and armed forces, the inhospitable terrain, and the lack of infrastructure. She just feels she has to work in a new place and make change possible. It paid off and led to a full-length community-based program now run through the NEN's Resource Centre at Chizami, in Phek district in Nagaland.

Then came NEN's seminal work, a study of women in armed-conflict situations. The study was undertaken by Rashmi Goswami, M.G. Sreekala, and Meghna Goswami. It was a baseline study initiated in 1998 to address the impact of protracted armed conflict on the lives of women. The study used the CEDAW convention as a yardstick to analyze fulfillment of state's obligation to women's equity in the context of armed conflict. "When you read the cases," says Monisha, "you are stunned by the brutality women experience in conflict situations—both by state and nonstate actors. Women are raped, tortured, and their children taken away from them. They are rendered widows and are forced to flee their farms and homes and live in refugee camps. They are not compensated for their losses and have little or no resources to rebuild their lives. Many of them are traumatized but receive no psychological counseling. This large-scale distress, she says, has many causative factors. First is the operation of the Armed Forces (Special Powers) Act and other draconian laws. Second, the redressal mechanism just doesn't work, as there is a lot of apathy. Then, there is the overall patriarchal domination, the absence of women in the peace processes as well as in general decision-making."

"We continue our struggle to educate the public on women's rights issue. We shall keep on exerting pressure on the government on issues of gender justice, as well as educate the public with poster campaigns, street plays and meets."

Her dog Nupi nuzzles against her legs. She picks up a tennis ball and throws it in the air. He jumps up to catch it in his mouth and carry it back for a repeat performance.

I want to know if she is a religious person. "I always found rituals rather bothersome. When I once told my mother this, she said, 'We'll then make sure you do your work with devotion. That will be your way of worship.' Her words have remained in my heart, and my work is my religion. I have never had the time to sit back and take stock of what I have done. I am training NGOs, helping them to organize themselves, and teach them how to garner funds and document their work. I feel my work is a drop in the ocean. It is still very much a man's world. A woman is not allowed to have her space, be herself, and realize her potential, and the irony is the women have been the cornerstone of stability in times of conflict. When violence is unleashed, the woman manages her home, her farm, and her children all alone, trying to bring order and sanity."

Monisha is deeply troubled by domestic violence, and NEN has helped innumerable victims with information on where to go for help and what precautions to take. "Unfortunately, the National and State Commission for Women have no teeth and not much can be done."

She refuses to name any particular woman that she admires. "I admire women who are determined and independent, who are capable of leading their own lives, travel freely, and have a lot of integrity."

***

Monisha's day begins at 4:30 in the morning. She lives alone in her Guwahati flat and sets about tidying it up. Then she goes for a brisk walk along the city's empty streets, greeting the dawn. Then she comes back and gets on the Internet, answering emails and writing out reports to network with international bodies. Breakfast is a boiled egg, a salad, a slice of bread, and a cup of tea. She prefers to wear *salwar kameez* and trousers to office, donning *mekhela chadors* at meetings. Office hours mean consultations, preparing project reports, and meeting people. She finally winds down at 5:30. After a frugal dinner of soup and boiled vegetables, she retires to bed by 10, in anticipation of yet another hectic day.

As the years pass by, Monisha discovers that she cannot take things easy. There is always the next meeting to attend, the next project to plan, and some little organizational detail that needs ironing out. Given a choice, she would love to be with her family and read a book, with Nupi curled up at her feet. But there is a lot of spirit in her still. At the end of our interview she shows me on her laptop the pictures of her holiday in Germany. She is pedaling away swiftly along a cycling track, racing ahead to complete 36 km. At 62, Monisha Behal is still a woman very much on the go.

11

Words for the Wronged:
Rita Chowdhury

A cold wind from the grey Brahmaputra whipped into novelist Rita Chowdhury's palatial house on the base of the Ramshah hills. That is why the domestic help scuttled around, bolting doors and windows. Nandita and I are ensconced in the living room. Its green walls are unadorned. There is an ornate sofa set with pea-green cushions pushed against the four walls. In the center is a bare table. The look seems deliberately impersonal, utilitarian, and lacking the feminine touch. And it is just as well, for the mistress of the house has no desire to prettify and decorate her surroundings. She has looked deep into the dark heart of life and seen truths that make her readers flinch. Her life is not about bone china and crystal objet d'art, gourmet meals, and pleasant socializing. You are not likely to find her in the kitchen, not if she can help it. Just as she can see the broad bosom of the Brahmaputra from the many windows of her home, she is witness to the wide confluence of humanity moving forward, stumbling, falling by the wayside, picking itself up, and pulled inexorably by the forces of history. And Rita keeps her lonely vigil—tracing this momentous journey in book after book, never missing a beat.

Indeed, Rita Chowdhury is a celebrated name in the Assamese literary firmament. Till date she has penned no less than 14 novels—powerful works like *Abirata Jatra* (1981), *Tirthabhumi* (1988), *Maha Jibonor Adharshila* (1993), *Nayana Tarali Sujata* (1996), *Papiya Torar Sadhu* (1998), and *Deu Langkhui* and *Makam*. She won the Sahitya Akademi Award in 2008 for her novel *Deu Langkhui*. She is also a poet and teaches political science in Cotton College. Her verse anthologies are *Xudoor Nakshatra, Banariya Batahar Xuhuri, Alop Pooharar Alop Andharar,* and *Boga Matir Tulaxi.* Her most recent novel is *Mayabritto.*

Rita walked in, clad in a brilliant blue *mekhela chador* and a wine-red cardigan. She has left her hair open; a small vermilion dot on her forehead and a string of black beads add to her attractiveness. We plunge into the session at once. "You became an activist from a young age," I started. "How did it all begin? Did your family have political discussions at the dining table?"

"Not at all," she said. "My parents were not politically inclined, and I don't remember if we had any such talk. But certain things happened that had a powerful impact on me. My father Birajananda Chowdhury was working in Arunachal Pradesh as an officer." Incidentally, he was my inspiration for founding of the Jatiya Raksha Vahini by me later on. "In 1971, he was sent on deputation to the Haflong Police Training Centre, as base superintendent. There I saw him training East Pakistani men in guerilla warfare. They were Sheikh Mujibur Rahman's Mukti Bahini cadres. These exercises filled me with curiosity and anticipation. I became aware of a larger world, where dramatic events were unfolding every minute."

"I was about 10 or 11-year-old at that time. I had a cousin, Keshav Narayan Chowdhury, who was general secretary of All Assam Students Union (AASU). He had taken part in the Language movement. I too was drawn to this mass movement against foreign nationals. I had heard about several mass movements throughout my childhood and adolescence. It was thus most natural for me to be drawn into the anti-foreigners agitation." "So was that how Rita Chowdhury, the rebel born?" I asked.

She gestured toward the table laden with plates of food. "Please eat first." Biting into a chocolate pastry, Nandita scribbled as Rita spoke. "I would call myself a fighter rather than a rebel. I am a nonconformist, an inborn fighter. I have this instinct to protect and protest, which goes right back to my childhood days. If my father so much as raised his voice when speaking to my mother, I would spring to her defence."

"You have often spoken of your sister's death as having a great effect on you."

"Yes, Rupa was my older sister. She passed away within three days of falling ill. The doctor said it was cerebral malaria. My sister was a warm, caring, sweet-natured girl who looked after me like a mother. When she died she was only in class V. I have brought her back to life as a fictional character in my work. Her death was devastating for all of us. I think my childhood ended the day she passed away. The world became dark, full of menace. The old certainties were gone. I had been an unruly, impulsive child and had found refuge in her calm presence. But when she was gone, it was as if I was alienated from the world and I escaped to the world of books. I read obsessively, as if to try and forget the grief that surrounded me. I read Bankim Chandra, Lakshminath Bezbarua, Sarat Chandra, Rabindranath Tagore, Jyoti Prasad Agarwala, Shankar, and Sankho Maharaj. Though I read to escape this world, the books gave me a vision of it, which helped me to fashion reality with words."

"But the real world kept its hold on you," I said. "This time you were not just a participant in the anti-foreigner's movement, you were a fugitive, hiding from the police. How did that come about?"

"It all started in the small, upper Assam town of Margherita, when I was a higher-secondary student. The agitation intrigued me, and I used to discuss it obsessively with my friends. We circulated some leaflets among ourselves and were looking for ways and means to play our parts. I was a member of the Asom Jatiyatabadi Yuba Chhatra Parishad, and I spread awareness among the people about the issues of the time. Looking back, I realize that I had been impulsive and immature at that time, without a clear idea of my role in this great movement. I was very emotional, and once I cut myself on my left hand and smeared the foreheads of my friends with blood marks as a symbolic pledge. I still have the scar to remind me about it."

"Then, as the agitation gathered strength in Margherita, the police came looking for me. That was the time I went into hiding for a year, staying under assumed names in different places, with families who were strangers. My own home was raided, my brothers interrogated about my whereabouts. My father Birajananda Chowdhury also turned absconder. For months, I had no news of home. I had to make do with the barest necessities and adjust to strange surroundings. Between moving from one safe house to another, there were long spells when I was bound within four walls, with absolutely nothing to do. It was then that I penned my first novel *Abirata Jatra*, which mirrored the drama, restlessness, heroism, anger, and uncertainty of those unforgettable years. After I completed it, I came to know that the Assam Sahitya Sabha had announced a contest for manuscripts based on the Assam Agitation. I sent it to them from my hideout, and it won the prize for best manuscript. For seven months I had no contact with my family. It was as if I had dropped off from the face of the earth. And yet, I was safe in all those houses where the families took me in. Nobody misbehaved with me or reported about me to the authorities. Finally, I was arrested in Silpukhuri, Guwahati, in the middle of a busy street. I was kept at the Guwahati Sadar Thana. They interrogated me for several days and nights. I was not allowed to sleep, to wash myself, or have any kind of privacy. I had to face whole groups of police officers who subjected me to a barrage of questions. They were extremely annoyed when I refused to answer them. They could not get a word out of me. I would sit on my hair and cover my face with a *gamocha* and close my eyes. Not a word escaped my lips. I would sleep on a table and was in the lock-up for two whole weeks. The police were furious with me. I was a mere girl, and yet, I had defied them by remaining silent. After two weeks, I was sent to Dibrugarh jail. The living conditions became worse. My father was kept in the next cell. The cells were dark, cramped, and stank of urine. Once, a drunk police officer started misbehaving with me. I stretched out my arms through the cell bars, grabbed him and battered him against the iron bars. The jail authorities were determined to break my spirit. I was shunted off to the men's police barracks. I was to spend a night there. I was deliberately exposed to great danger. What could I, a lone woman, do if they attacked and raped me? I sat on a bed in the barracks, wide awake, ready to strike if anyone tried anything. But the men were so gallant. They told me not to worry, talked to me, and even got me *chapatti-sabzi* from the canteen. After that I was transferred to Guwahati Jail again and finally released. I had been arrested twice in Guwahati and once in Dibrugarh."

"The next milestone in your life was your marriage to politician Chandra Mohan Patowary," I said. "As a politician's wife there is a lot of uncertainty, pressures of both success and failure. There was also the security issue. He has been the cabinet minister of the Asom Gana Parishad (AGP) government for two terms and is now president of the AGP."

"Yes, strangely, for 10 years after *Abirata Jatra* I did not write anything. I was under a spell of confusion. Confusion regarding my identity, my place in the world, and the kind of work I wanted to do. After a lot of soul-searching, I knew I had to go back among the people because that was where I belonged. And I realized I would have to do it by exploring the joys, sorrows, hopes, and fears of the people through literature. Interestingly, the period of my creative hiatus corresponded to the nine years of my marriage when I was unable to conceive. In those years I saw the cruelty with which society treated a childless woman. And when my daughter was born, I began to write again, and in a sense, I was born with her again."

Do you see yourself as a good wife and mother? I was keen to know.

"Well," she smiles fleetingly. "I am a wife who is very conscious of her rights. I see myself as a responsible wife who also plays the role of a mother to my husband. But I am not one for slipping into the mould of the traditional housewife, and I have never spent time cooking and decorating the home. I never nag my husband and give him enough space. Motherhood occupies top priority in my life. I think I am a good mother, but I could have done more. I wish I had spent more time with my son and daughter, instead of having to keep away due to other responsibilities."

Rita is at her most eloquent when she talks of writing. "As a writer, I try to break out of the limitations of being a woman. I have deliberately attempted to not be conscious of the gender identity, and I never feel the need to assert myself as a woman when I write. That is why you will find the humanist rather than the feminist in my work."

What drives me to write is to break out of the shackles of a body-centric existence. I need to ascend from the trivialities of everyday life. Writing for me is not the achievement of fame but a way of giving back something meaningful to the world. That is why, even though I wrote a few romantic novels in the beginning, I later became much more selective in my themes, writing about great issues and entire communities. I am always hopeful that my books will bring positive change in the lives of the marginalized and voiceless people I write about. Writing is a responsible art because many readers believe in my words. I could write powerfully and convincingly about a protagonist who commits suicide, but its impact on a reader could be destructive. But I cannot pretend that my books offer any answers. They only present a true picture. The reader has to take it forward from there."

"I do not fear controversy," she shrugged. "If I think it is right, then nothing can stop me from writing it. When I wrote *Makam*, about the fate of the Chinese uprooted from Makum after the Indo-China war of 1962, a series of letters appeared in a vernacular paper, condemning me for being anti-India and pro-China. My novel *Popiya Torar Sadhu*, which tells the true story of a young aspiring journalist and her ruthless exploitation by certain men, leading to her tragic suicide, did not receive a single review in any newspaper or magazine. My novel *Deu Langkhui* was written after a lot of soul-searching. I knew that writing it could lead to ugly confrontations between the Tiwas and Kacharis. So I chose a veiled character, someone who did not belong to these groups, as the mischief monger."

"Writing is my brand of activism. I have been asked whether I have been influenced by Mahasweta Devi who wrote about the tribals and gave voice to their problems. But I have not been influenced by any particular author. The act of writing is painful to me; I have to do it because many unknown stories need to be told. So I have my corner, my space where I weave my tales, but I also go out frequently to the world to gather the materials I need to write."

"What are the special challenges of penning historical fiction?" Nandita asks.

"The greatest challenge is that there has to be a smooth, seamless blending between fact and fiction. In many such works, the two realms run parallel to each other, without meeting, which proves counterproductive. Another vital aspect is the use of words. Words reflect time. You should be conscious about the fact as to whether certain words were used during that particular time frame. It is also important to be specific about clothes, jewelry, household artifacts, weapons, and tools used by people of that period. While writing *Deu Langkhui*, I had absolutely no written chronicles and had to rely on oral history for research."

Rita's son comes to the room, anxiety writ large on his face. He needs to get a number of things from the market for his school project and asks her permission to take the car. Now her attention is on him, his problem, and we wrap up the session for the day. Outside, darkness shrouds the great river, but the bone-chilling wind whips around, an unrelenting spirit. We hug, promising to meet, and Nandita and I clamber into the car. Before we back out of the drive, Rita is already walking briskly back to her house, without a backward glance.

***

Rita Chowdhury's life has seen many trials and tribulations. The blow of her beloved sister's death causes her to still weep when talking about her. As a teenager, she has spent long, uncertain spells away from home, caught up in the cause she believed in with all her heart. Later she got two postgraduate degrees, one in Assamese and another in political science, as well as a doctorate degree in political science, and again, a degree in law. As a writer her canvas has been vast, her themes complex, and narrative many-layered. She has also been the wife of a politician, playing this difficult role even while staying removed from his political affiliations, trying to lead a normal life surrounded by security men and the trappings of a VIP existence. In all the years I have known her, Rita has always seemed to me to be a woman of tremendous resilience. No wonder then that she identifies herself with the character of Tejimola, a beloved heroine of Assamese folklore. In order to understand why, one has to know this story, narrated by countless grandmothers to wide-eyed children in the moonlit courtyards of Assamese homes. It goes like this. A merchant has two wives and a daughter named Tejimola. When the elder wife dies, the stepmother is put in charge of the girl. The merchant goes abroad. Tejimola wishes to attend a friend's wedding. Her stepmother gives her a bundle of clothes to wear at the wedding. When Tejimola opens the bundle, she finds a mouse and cinders, with the clothes quite ruined. She comes home weeping and is thrashed by her step mother. Then she is made to help in the husking of paddy. Her right hand is crushed under the tooth of the husking pedal. She is then forced to use her left hand, which is also crushed. Then it is her feet that are crushed. After her head is smashed, the stepmother hurries to hide her body under the eaves of the hut where the husking pedal stands. By and by a gourd vine grows on the roof of the hut. When a beggar woman tries to pick a gourd, it cries, "Stop! I am Tejimola and have been killed by my stepmother!" On hearing this, the stepmother chops the vine and flings it away. A tree with sour fruits springs up where it falls. When cowherds come to pluck its fruits, the voice of Tejimola cries out again. This time the tree is cut and thrown into the river. There it grows into a beautiful lotus. Now the merchant returns and sees the lotus. He at once wants it as a gift for his daughter Tejimola. When his boatman stretches out his hand to pluck it, the voice of Tejimola cries out loud. The merchant is astonished. He takes a bit of areca nut in one hand, and a sweet ball on the other and says, "If you are indeed my Tejimola, change into a *salika* (bird *myna*) and take these areca nut pieces, and if not, take this sweet ball." Heeding his words, the lotus changed into a *myna* and bit the areca nut. The merchant puts the bird in a cage, comes home, and asks about his daughter. The stepmother is forced to tell the truth. The merchant throws a kerchief over the cage and says, "If you are indeed my daughter, change into your own shape." Tejimola returns to her old form and the wicked stepmother is driven out.

What appeals to Rita is the indestructible nature of Tejimola. She survives the most dreadful persecution and emerges in a new form every time. She will not be silenced. Her voice rises to defy her tormentor and her fate. What interests Rita is the story of people caught in the vice-like grip of circumstances, people rising up to meet something greater than their circumscribed individual selves, bravely resisting injustice.

One such milestone in Rita's life and the larger life of Assamese nationalism was the movement that began in 1979. But the causes of the movement date as far back as 1826. In our next session with Rita, we sit at a city restaurant specializing in authentic Assamese cuisine. The whole place has been done up in bamboo, the seats too are of hollow bamboo logs, and red tasseled Chinese lanterns emit a dim glow in the dark interior. We have steamed rice with duck curry, dry fish chutney, roasted tomato mash, pork cooked with lai greens, and crisp fingerlings fried with onions and chilies. The meal over, Rita is in the right mood for a history lesson and the teacher in her takes over. "You see, Assam was never politically integrated with the North Indian empires before the arrival of the British. When the British took over Assam after the Treaty of Yandaboo in 1826, it was the end of 400 years of freedom. The British East India Company had its headquarters in Calcutta, and they slowly gained controlled over the entire Northeast. So much so that as early as 1838 Assam was made part of the Bengal Presidency. In 1978, MLA Hiralal Patowary died, requiring a by-election to the Mangaldoi Lok Sabha constituency to fill his seat. During the process of the election, observers noticed that the number of registered voters had grown dramatically. The AASU demanded that elections be postponed till names of foreign nationals were deleted from the rolls. Then Assam was separated from Bengal in 1874 and brought under the control of a Chief Commissioner stationed in Shillong, which was to be its capital. Sylhet district, populated mainly by Bengali Muslims, was now a part of Assam. You have to understand certain demographic changes deliberately brought about by the British that had very serious effects later. First, they prevented the natural assimilation of various tribes into mainstream Assamese society. Secondly, they brought thousands of tribal laborers from Central India to work in their tea estates. These people were kept apart from the local populace and tension simmered among them. Then they brought in lakhs of Bengali peasants (mainly Muslims) to settle in the riverine tracts and grow crops there. There began a deluge of these people who claimed land as their own, cleared vast tracts of jungle, and antagonized the local population. As the years passed, they spread to upper Assam. The demography of Assam again saw rapid changes during partition when refugees flooded to the state from East Pakistan."

In this way the religious and linguistic composition changed drastically. The local Assamese people feared they would be turned into a minority in their own land. Thus began the struggle for Assamese identity. The *Asomiya*s found themselves underrepresented in the services and professions. After partition, however, the Hindu middle class were in power after 150 years. Now they tried to establish their cultural identity and seek economic and social equality. In 1972 the AASU launched the *Bhasa Andolan* or Language Movement to make *Asomiya* language as the medium of instruction up to graduate level in addition to English. The state government took measures to do so. Unfortunately, violent riots targeting Bengalis broke out. Both Hindu and Muslim Bengalis were victims. But migration to the state continued.

"Yes, and the flash point was reached in 1979," remarked Nandita, poring over her notes.

"Yes. The Government of India stipulated that elections for the Assam State Legislative Assembly and 12 unfilled parliamentary seats would be held from February 14 to 21. The AASU and the AGP declared that they would boycott the elections, the reason given being that the electoral lists contained names of thousands of illegal migrants who were not bonafide Indian citizens. Allowing them to the vote would automatically confer citizen rights on them. The demand was that all who entered the state from Bangladesh after 1961 be expelled and names deleted from the electoral rolls. What was very disturbing was that the number of registered voters had gone up from 6.3 million in 1972 to 8.7 million in 1979. After many talks, the Government of India agreed to March 1971 as the cutoff date. Later, Indira Gandhi called the elections, which AASU and AGP were keen to boycott. The Bengali Hindus and Muslims wanted to vote. The elections were also supported by Plains Tribal Class of Assam, comprising of Bodos who wanted autonomy."

"In 1979, Assam witnessed widespread unrest. Bridges were burnt down, and schools, colleges, and offices were forcibly closed. Thousands of state government employees refused to take part in poll duty, and disciplinary action was taken against them, including arrests and suspensions. Bodo tribals attacked Assamese peasants at Gohpur. But what was truly tragic was what happened in Nellie, a region along the south bank of the Brahmaputra. Mobs of Lalungs and Assamese attacked the village of Nellie with swords, guns, sticks, and axes. On February 12, 1983, 1,200 men, women, and children died in Nellie. There was another massacre at Chaulkhowa Chapari in Darrang district and Silapathar in Lakhimpur district. Thousands of people poured into relief camps. Hundreds fled to West Bengal. Elections could not be completed in 16 out of 126 constituencies. In one constituency a candidate was even murdered. Voters turnout was high in the Bengali-dominated states and low in others. Indira Gandhi's Congress party won 90 out of 108, but the boycott was successful."

The agitation continued for five years and ended with the signing of the Assam Accord in 1985. The Parliament passed the Illegal Migrants Determination by Tribunal Act for detection of foreigners settled in Assam. In 1985, the AGP, which had played a leading role in the movement, came to power.

The succeeding years would see the rise of insurgency in Assam, and the failure of the youth leaders to hold the reins of power. Rita's engagement with the foreigners' movement would be explored by her in two more novels. But something new caught her attention. As a young girl she had heard of Chinese people settled in Makum, a small semi-urban habitat known for its tea and oil industry in Upper Assam. She unearthed the sad chronicle of humble people, law-abiding citizens subjected to tragic displacement and loss. The forefathers of the Chinese had been brought from China to work in the tea gardens by the British in the early

19th century. With the passage of time, their children and grand-children integrated with the local community by marriage. Many of them also started other enterprises rather than working in the tea gardens. Their safe little world collapsed when the Indo-China war broke out in 1962. On November 10 of that year, 1,500 Assamese Chinese were cruelly rounded up and packed off to congested internment camps at Deoli in Rajasthan before being deported. Almost immediately, the government auctioned their properties. Families were separated, parents from children, and husbands from wives. Today these exiled people live in Hong Kong and in many places around the world. They suffer in silence and long to visit Assam. The trauma of that episode is very much evident among them and there is a need for closure. Rita Chowdhury wants the Indian Government to apologize for this injustice and condemns how a country could turn against its own citizens.

"There were no written materials on what took place in Makum," explains Rita Chowdhury. "It was as if there was a conspiracy of silence. The victim themselves were terrified of baring the truth and angering the authorities. Many of them were old and their memories of those dark days were fading. Nearly a year went by with me trying to win their confidence. I went to South China and, with the help of people whose names I cannot disclose, was able to locate many families who had been separated, displaced, and uprooted. Slowly, as I visited their homes; they opened up and revealed the heartbreak they have had to endure all these years. They spoke in Assamese; they talked of Assamese customs, festivals, food items, and the places they had called home. They brought out old, yellowing letters from loved ones, faded photographs. Tears flowed freely. More than anger it was sadness that was evident on these occasions. They had passed a lifetime of parting and sorrow. Who would ever be able to compensate for that? In their new country China, where they settled after the events of 1962, there had been many difficulties and problems of adjustment.

But they are unwilling to speak about that for fear of antagonizing the authorities."

"Ultimately, it was the three Chinese gentlemen from London, Nepal, and Singapore who joined the pieces of the jigsaw puzzle of this momentous event and gave me the perspective needed to pen this saga. When I wrote this book, I had to read about war, the tea industry, history, and Chinese culture. Since there were gaps in the chronology of events I had to rely on my imagination. In the end I used about only 20 percent of my research material. *Makam* was my most ambitious book. It became my mission, and I was driven to tell this riveting story. *Makam* transformed me in many ways. Before writing the book I was a normal woman with limited concerns. *Makam* broadened my horizons, made me rise above trivialities, and reach for that which is noble and eternal in life."

Rita keeps going back to the stirring days of the Assam movement, which changed the direction of her live in momentous ways. "I began to realize the existence of a greater life, something higher than one's personal concerns of daily existence. Spending months in jail, traveling in police vans, hiding in exile . . . these are times which shaped me, made me who I am today. Those difficult days freed me from all earthly desires, so that I am indifferent to material possessions. The movement ended, but I continued my search for a greater life, this time through my writing. Freedom is very dear to me, and I abhor any form of confinement. I refuse to the defined by my husband's political affiliations. But I am not a fixed entity. I too am evolving, and you may notice that through several books I look back on the Assam Agitation through subtly shifting perspectives. My first novel *Abirata Jatra* (1981) covered the frenzy of the uprising and the brutality of the army toward the common people. Mariam was my alter ego; Prithivi, Joseph, and Samudra Phukan were born of my own experiences among fellow activists. *Tirtha Bhumi* (1988) looks back on the movement after its six-year period. In *Mahajibonar Adharshila* (1993), I tried to focus on the frustration and stagnation of the Assamese youth after the movement and the many repercussions they had to cope with. There is a clear disillusionment, a sense of a dream turning sour. Then in *Ei Samay, Xei Samay* there is a calm and objective evaluation of those eventful years, an examination of its ideology, and the course it followed."

It is not merely contemporary history that Rita Chowdhury is adept in. Her gaze extends far back to the days of hoary antiquity, creating a fascinating world of real, believable characters of an age for removed from our own. Her Sahitya Akademi Award–winning novel, *Deu Langkhui*, can be read as a gripping story of the characters Jongal Balahu, Arimatta, Gangawat, Chandraprabha, and others. It can be read as a historical novel revealing facts about the Tiwas and the Ahoms. It can also be interpreted as a feminist chronicle mirroring the life of Chandraprabha. Chandraprabha, queen of Pratap Singha, is friendly toward the Gobha Raja at the Jonbeel Mela. The jealous king banishes her to the Gobha kingdom. The Gobha Raja acts with honor and does not take advantage of her. The wronged queen familiarizes herself with the local customs and gives up her former identity. The story-telling is vivid, the prose subtle, and the effortlessness conceals the painstaking research that she undertook before penning this wonderful saga.

After the release of *Mayabritto*, which is a complex novel with philosophical explorations, Rita Chowdhury surprised everyone by hinting that it could well be her last work. But to practice any art is to make the soul grow, and Rita would surely not limit her evolvement at the peak of her creative phase. As she has herself admitted, honoring her calling is her way of feeling most truly alive. She is wise not to be trapped by dogma and never lets out other voices drown out her own. In the end, you realize that this solemn woman with her watchful eyes is among the fortunate people who have found a calling that is bigger than they are, a calling that moves them and fills their lives with constant passion and growth.

12
Director's Special: Manju Borah

It is a wet monsoon afternoon. Raindrops quiver on each leaf on the potted plants at filmmaker Manju Borah's cozy office verandah. The single-story house is where Manju Borah conceives of her cinematic projects and struggles to give their final form. In another part of the city, Manju Borah has a home where she is a wife, a daughter-in-law, and a housewife. In that home she cooks delicious dishes, decorates the living room, and pours her police officer husband his tea when he returns home from work. In this neatly compartmentalized life, Manju plays her many roles with sincerity and pragmatism. I had interviewed Manju Borah in 1999, just after her first film *Baibhab*, which was a dark, haunting film lauded both by critics and discerning cinegoers. She has gone on to direct seven more films, winning awards like the Silver Lotus Award for *Baibhab* on 47th National Film Awards, Best Feature Film in Assamese for *Akashitorar Kothare* on 51st National Film Awards, National Film Award 2008 for best feature film on national integration for *Aai Kot Nai*, Satyajit Ray Memorial Award 2012 by the Third Eye Asian Film Festival of Mumbai, and the National Film Award 2012 for the Best Feature Film in Mishing for *Ko: Yad*. Mounted on the walls of her office are the various citations, posters of her films, and photographs of her on stage to receive awards. The bookcases are crammed with trophies and awards. But Manju Borah is too grounded, too sensible, to feel the euphoria of her success. Plump, pleasant, and direct in her speech, she readily admits to having quite a temper when things don't go her way on the sets.

"It is definitely an advantage to be a story writer and a film-maker. Being a writer myself, I understand what narrative is all about. But film is far more powerful, as it is a visual art. A writer interacts with a reader on a one-to-one, intimate basis. But the reach of cinema is immense. There is a captive audience taking in the experience. Then again, I write in Assamese. The language limits the readership. But the beauty of cinema is that it transcends the barriers of language. As an art form, it is extremely interesting and challenging. There is a temptation to use my own stories in my films. My pet themes include the dynamics of the man–woman relationship and the unplumbed depths of a woman's heart. But it was clear that I cannot keep repeating my pet themes in film after film. That is why I am compelled to take stories from others. As regional filmmakers, we work under a lot of restraints. Finance is always a worrying factor. In such a situation, a filmmaker ponders on the relevance and significance of a story that he or she sets out to film. Filming for us is never an idle, self-indulgent pastime."

So who are the filmmakers she admires? She puckers her brow, deep in thought. Then she says, "I would say Ritwik Ghatak, Satyajit Ray, Jahnu Barua, Frederico Fellini, and Tarkovsky. Ghatak's cinematic treatment of his material is unique. His work reflects his times and the camerawork is fantastic. Satyajit Ray's *Pather Panchali* is a movie far ahead of its times. It was made when mythology still ruled Indian cinema. Jahnu Barua has the gift of conveying in a very simple way some powerful truths of life. I enjoy Fellini's earlier films, which were relatively simple. Then, the later films like *8½* dare to play with ideas and the effect is daz-zling. The canvas of Tarkovsky is spectacular. His films help you understand all the twists and turns of Russian history. I have also been deeply influenced by the French New Wave film director Robert Bresson who laid great emphasis on using nonprofessional actors. I tried his technique in *Ko: Yad*, where Mishing people played all the key roles and was thus able to attain a very natural feel. I held workshops with these people before shooting. Bresson also showed the darker face of society, which appealed to me. Some of my critics say that my films do not entertain. So be it. What, after all, is entertainment? It means to stimulate, to create a spark in the mind, and to provoke one to think. My films attempt to do this, don't they? Cinema is a powerful medium. You have to do more than sing and dance around trees. You have to leave a piece of art that will outlive its time."

Movie making is grueling business. Manju believes that order and discipline are key to getting things done. Everything is planned to the last detail. But before the actual shoot, she spends enough time with the story, exploring it, developing it, right up to the moment she falls in love with it. Over the years she has created a team of artists and technicians who understand her style of functioning.

"The biggest challenge in filmmaking is finding your audience. Previously, parallel cinema had a platform. Not anymore. Mainstream cinema is exploring unusual themes in a bid to attract audiences. Thanks to the Internet, we have access to world cinema and cine societies have become redundant. Sadly, Indian filmmakers are fond of copying ideas, scenes and so on from foreign films. These days, thankfully, it is getting tougher to do that. So we have an audience that is exposed to the best in world cinema. It is a challenge to come up with something new."

So, what is a trademark Manju Borah film? She laughs and replies, "My films are rooted in the reality of Northeast. Through cinema I give voice to all our concerns. My films try to mirror the complexity of our existence as well as the culture and belief systems that are unique to us."

Manju Borah is among the handful of women who have worked as directors in the Assamese film industry, and the others include Suprabha Devi and Santwana Bordoloi. Assamese cinema was born in 1935 when Jyoti Prasad Agarwala released his film *Joymoti*. The industry has developed over the years, witnessing critical and artistic success, with filmmakers of the stature of Bhabendranath Saikia and Jahnu Barua achieving national and international recognition. But the industry has been unable to make a breakthrough in the national scene, though several films have bagged National Awards over the years. Overshadowed by Bollywood, it has started making Bollywood type of films to stay afloat. Many significant sociopolitical factors have played a part in its gradual decline. The six-year long anti-foreigners agitation dealt a body blow, when the masses stopped going to movie halls. Later, insurgents announced a boycott of Hindi films. Bereft of audiences, many cinema halls closed down, and the remaining ones went to seed. Manju strongly feels that building cineplexes is not the answer. She also rues the fact that with the multiplicity of dialects, there is always only a small fraction of people who will watch an Assamese film.

But Manju Borah remains upbeat about the industry. She loves it with rare passion. Her early life is also a faithful source of inspiration. "I was born and brought up in a village. We were always excited by the many festivals like Bihu, Raas, and plays that were organized for our enjoyment. The village library was maintained by the youth and was seen as a precious asset. I did not act and sing, but read gems of Indian and world literature. I was an avid moviegoer and did not miss a single movie show at a nearby theater. During Kali Puja and Durga Puja, there would be screenings of films near our house."

Manju Borah made her foray into cinema in 1999 with her film *Baibhab*, revealing a quiet sophistication and finely honed aesthetic sense. The story revolves around the 37-year-old Samiran Chowdhury, an academic and poet who is haunted by his brother's death, caused when he had, as a child, knocked him down with his bicycle. Even as his marriage unravels, he finds companion-ship through another woman. His sense of alienation and guilt is heightened when his father is arrested for corruption. Samiran ultimately retires to a village to discover his roots and find peace.

The central character is an unlikely hero, and the film skill-fully delves into his fractured psyche. The character's vulnerability strikes a chord in the audience. The film was awarded Jury's Special Mention in the 47th National Film Festival 2000 and was also rec-ognized as the Best Film in Asia at the 6th Dhaka International Film Festival, 2000.

Her next film *Anya Ek Yatra*, repeats the motif of the tortured chief protagonist. But unlike the passivity of Samiran in *Baibhab*, Vikram is ready to stake all to help his doctor father set up a xenotransplantation clinic, by robbing a bank with the help of an extremist gang.

But it was her next film *Akashitorar Kothare* (A tale told a thou-sand times) that reflected Borah's feminist leanings. She talks about the film. "Women have had to make many sacrifices. In our own society, the sacrifices of Sati Beula, Sati Joymoti, the folklore of Kamala Kumari, the customs of Hudum Puja of the Rajbongshis, the Kherai Puja of the Bodos, Kumari Puja, and the sacrifices of the Devadasis are well-known examples. In a country where god-desses are worshipped for their strength, virtue, and learning, real-ity is just the opposite. Even in the educated and affluent section of society, women are deprived of their rightful place and are forced to live like caged birds."

"The story of *Akashitorar Kothare* is familiar to millions of women around the world. She is highly educated, talented, and ambitious. But when she marries Raghab Chowdhury, an IAS officer, her life takes a nose dive. She is seen as a trophy wife and is expected to give up her research work. In such a scenario, her marriage stifles her, and the claustrophobia leads to tragic results. Even years later, I get calls from women to say how their lives are similar to *Akashitorar Kothare*. My cinematographer Arun Bose was so moved when he was doing this film that he went home and asked his wife if there was anything she would like to do besides looking after the home and family.

Akashitorar Kothare won the National Award for the Best Regional Feature Film and State Award for Best Director along with the Best Audience Award at the Dacca International Film Festival in 2004.

Akashitorar Kothare was about a privileged woman of a certain class. Manju Borah's next film *Laaj* was uncompromising in its pitiless gaze on the miserable existence of the rural poor, afflicted by poverty, disease, ignorance, and superstition. Ila, the protagonist of the film *Laaj*, represents this society. She is a girl who is fighting against insurmountable odds to complete her education. She belongs to a poor fishing community that is ostracized by the so-called high-caste people. Every single day is a battle against prejudice, hunger, ignorance, and despair. Ila's ultimate shame is not having an undergarment to go to school. Is not Ila's shame the shame of entire humanity? *Laaj* was selected for Indian Panorama and other festivals, apart from winning awards, in 2004.

You never quite know where Manju is going to seek her inspiration from. From the claustrophobic middle-class existence of *Akashitorar Kothare* to the half-clad village girl, Manju turned her gaze to history. She now busied herself in portraying a valiant Ahom princess who has long been regarded as an emblem of self-sacrifice. Joymoti sacrificed her life, cruelly tortured in the fields of Jerenga, so that the upheavals caused by corrupt officials like Laluksola Borphukan might end and her husband Gadadhar Singha, having fled to the Naga hills, might return to power. The Ahom kings, starting with Sukapha who invaded Assam from Burma, in the 13th century, ruled Assam for 600 years. When the political, social, and cultural life of a nation is threatened, a savior emerges to solve the crisis. During the black period of Ahom rule (1670–1681), when as many as seven kings had either committed suicide or were poisoned, the plight of the common man was pitiable.

"I do not see Joymoti as a victim or as a woman merely sacrificing her life for her husband. I have shown her as a political power. She knew what she was doing and had the vision to understand what was happening. She was a brave woman who was prepared to pay the ultimate price. Instead of pity for her tragic predicament, I have tried to evoke admiration and inspiration."

In her next film *Aai Kot Nai*, Manju returns to contemporary reality. "We all know the long border conflict between Assam and Nagaland. Nagaland is itself fighting for sovereignty. For decades villagers on both sides have attacked and killed each other, burnt homes, and destroyed crops. These skirmishes are so common that they don't even merit the front page of newspapers as news. In my film *Aai Kot Nai*, I have shown that in spite of the hostility, the mutual suspicion, and bad blood, human beings are capable of reaching out to each other. An Assamese boy and a Naga girl fall in love. The return of a small baby by a compassionate woman belonging to another community is a ray of light in the darkness." Looking into a little-explored saga of present-day history, Manju weaves a tale of love and redemption. For this she was honored with the Nargis Dutt Award for Best Feature Film on National Integration in the 56th National Film Awards 2008.

Now it was time to move into new territory. She got down to making a film in the Mishing language. The Mishing are the largest tribal group in Northeast India. For the film, she camped with her team in a remote, flood-prone Mishing village and held acting workshops involving the villagers. When they lost all self-consciousness in facing the camera, she began to shoot. "*Ko: Yad* is a tale of desperation told through Pokkam, as he faces life's many betrayals. Given a beating by his father when he comes of age, he makes his living by collecting firewood from the surging Brahmaputra. The film traces his life from childhood, marriage, and the birth of his children, through his old age as he hails thanklessly for his family and is faced with the betrayal of his friends, his creditors, his children, and ultimately, the river itself. It is a tale of suffering, and I have dealt with it as honestly as possible, without doling out false hope."

Now we come to how Manju has evolved as a director. Each film brings with it new experiences and new challenges. "Having no institutional training in my craft, I have to, as they say, play it by the ear. I constantly try to learn different aspects of filmmaking—camera angles, costume, music, dubbing . . . and whatever I also read widely, books on literature and philosophy, which broaden my outlook. My earliest training came from watching films and discussing them with my friends, though there was no film society either in Jorhat or Shillong, where I studied. But I was privileged to watch movies like *Bridge on the River Kwai* and *Gone with the Wind*. I assisted Rajen Rajkhowa in the making of his television serial *Pothorughate Ringiyai*. Through him I came in contact with Verity Lambert, a BBC Channel 4 producer who was in India to make *A Suitable Boy*, a film based on Vikram Seth's novel with the same title. That film never got made, but as her Delhi coordinator I learnt the thoroughness with which they conducted research. Then I was chief assistant director to Rajen Rajkhowa in *Sopon*. I learnt all the practical aspects of filmmaking. I was by now growing more confident of directing my own film. This was the time I met cinematographer Mrinal Kanti Das, who had already won accolades for *Adajya* and *Raag Biraag*. We soon became a team, along with sound engineer Jatin Sarma, who had worked under David Lean."

"Certainly there were problems initially. My lead actor Ashok Medhi in *Baibhab* fell ill and returned to America. That held up shooting for a year. People laughed and passed comments. Then, during shooting, the cameramen and technicians tried to have things their way. I also learnt that as a director you must do your script yourself, even if it is not your own story."

Talking about her favorite characters in her films, Manju says, "Among the women Joymoti is my favorite. I have projected her as not just a devoted, tortured wife but a martyr choosing to sacrifice her life for the good of the Ahom kingdom. Samiran Chowdhury of *Baibhab* is very dear to me. He may appear to you as a weak man consumed by guilt and haunted by his past, but in the need, he takes the bold step of acknowledging that he is a part of his father's wrongdoing."

For her the hardest part of filmmaking is not okaying the shots, motivating the actors or checking for continuity. It is choosing a subject and growing with it. "When a story appeals to me, I spend months pondering over it, expanding it, and exploring it from all angles. Sometimes, after the initial euphoria, I hit a roadblock. Then I have to look for something else." However starved she is of subjects at times, she will never make films where couples go dancing around trees and scantily clad girls dance in bars.

Manju Borah has a number of telefilms, teleserials, and documentaries to her credit. She holds responsible positions in different cine-organizations. To name a few she is the chairman of the Joint Advisory Committee of Eastern India Motion Picture Association and also a member of the script panel of National Film Development Corporation Limited. She has served as Jury Member of Feature Films, Indian Panorama, IFFI 2007, 55th National Film Award, 2007, 10th MAMI International Film Festival 2008, and 3rd Eye 7th Asian Film Festival Mumbai 2008. As a jury member, she tries to be as unbiased and fair as possible and the work of other filmmakers gives her insight into their style of approaching cinema. One of the most valuable lessons that she learnt from officiating as a jury member is that films must have the integrity to reflect the reality of the places they inaugurate in. Through all her eight films, Manju has kept this dictum in mind.

Now we turn to the other roles that Manju plays with equal commitment. "I think I am a very good wife," she asserts with conviction. "I am not just Dilip's wife but also his friend. I cook the dishes he loves and take care of his clothes. When I am not shooting I always reach home earlier so that I am there when he comes back from work. As an IPS officer he is under a lot of stress, and I make sure he relaxes with me. I am very tolerant and broad-minded. As a mother, I have been very liberal. I have some differences of opinion with my daughter, but my son admires my work as he is a keen movie buff."

Manju generously offers tips to debutant filmmakers. "You must be thorough in your homework. You must communicate closely with the main character at least two months in advance. This is most important to build a rapport with them. It is also important to plan the music carefully. Each film demands its own kind of camera work. You must have a vision of the film you are going to make. Filmmaking is an expensive and extremely taxing profession. If you have nothing meaningful to say, don't waste your time and money."

That is Manju Borah for you—up front and never mincing her words. Several national awards and international recognition have not changed her in the least. Warm and accessible, she refuses to launch into abstract theorizing of her work. For her, the hands-on approach has always worked the best. She is quietly involved into another new project, an animated film on Assam's saint reformer Sankaradeva, which is meant for young audiences. For her, it is much more than a film. It is the beginning, as always, of a new discovery.

Index

About the Author

Indrani Raimedhi is a journalist, a columnist, and an author. She won the Kunjabala Devi Award for Investigative Reporting on women issues in 2004. She is at present Feature Editor with the *Assam Tribune* daily (established 1939) and was recruited as the first woman journalist in the editorial department in 1989. Author of nine books, Raimedhi's four anthologies of short stories include *The Season Coming*, *The Concubine's Room*, *The Night Journey*, and *The Stranger's Touch*. Her books for children have been used in schools as rapid readers. Her poetry and short fiction have been published in national magazines as well as in Austria and The Netherlands. Raimedhi has been Resource Person at IGNOUs Phone-in-Creative Writing Program in All India Radio, Guwahati. Several of her stories have been translated and also made into television serials.

She has researched and anchored a six-part series on Assam's greatest living writers. She has visited Germany, Belgium, and UK as a delegate of an AINEF—European Union Gender Project. At present she is giving the finishing touches to another anthology of short fictions titled *A Season of Waiting*.